Help!

For Parents of Children from Ages Six to Twelve Years

By Parents for Parents

Vol. 5
The Suggestion Circle Series

Edited by

Jean Illsley Clarke,
Deane Gradous,
Sandra Sittko, M.S.W.,
and Christine Ternand, M.D.

1817

Harper & Row, Publishers, San Francisco

Cambridge, Hagerstown, New York, Philadelphia, Washington,
London, Mexico City, Sao Paulo, Singapore, Sydney

*To all the children of all the parents
who shared their wisdom for this book.*

The developmental affirmations for children on pages
14 to 18 are adapted from Pamela Levin's therapeutic
affirmations in *Becoming the Way We Are* and are used
with the permission of the author.

Cover design: Terry Dugan
Illustrations: Jerry Smath

Library of Congress Cataloging-in-Publication Data

Help! for parents of children ages six to twelve years.

(The Suggestion circle series ; vol. 5)
Includes index.
1. Child rearing—United States. 2. Children—
Care and hygiene—United States. I. Clarke, Jean
Illsley. II. Parents for parents. III. Series.
HQ772.H42   1986   649'.124   86-18381
ISBN 0-86683-455-9

86 87 88 89 90 OPM 10 9 8 7 6 5 4 3 2 1

Contents

CLUSTERS AND SUGGESTION CIRCLES

Appreciations

We offer our appreciations to

- The many people who shared their wisdom in these circles. Without them this book would not exist.
- Lois White and Lillian Weger, A.C.S.W., for their careful reading of the manuscript and for their many helpful suggestions.
- Joanne Smith, Glenn Smith, Roxanne Michelson, Sandee Goldsmith, Sheri Goldsmith, Ron Kubes, Kay Kubes, Mary Kay Truitt, Susan K. Keane, Rosemarie Zawacki, and Margaret Molyko, for their special efforts.
- Peter Geittmann, for his support.
- Paul Singh and the pediatricians at St. Paul Group Health Medical Center, for their support.
- Bobbi Mlekodaj, for her help at the beginning of this book.
- William and Phyllis Sittko, David and Diana Sittko, Deborah, Timothy, and Susan Sittko, for their ideas and support.
- Doug and Fred and Dick, for ongoing support and to Alex, Eric, Allen, Susan, Marc, Jennifer, and Wade for teaching us about children on the home front.
- Becky Monson, Nancy Nenovich, Mary Ann Lisk, and Vivian Rouson-Gossett, for their support, encouragement, and dedicated typing.
- Pat Lassonde, for her helpful editing and continuous encouragement.

—The Editors

Foreword

As an elementary school teacher, a facilitator of "Self-Esteem: A Family Affair" classes, and a parent who has improved her ways of parenting, I want to share with you my excitement about this book and about the powerful Suggestion Circle technique it employs to help parents. Children, between the ages of six and twelve, use their experiences to make decisions that affect how they will handle their important teenage and adult years.

With this book, parents and teachers will find ways to give kids the important information and guidance they'll need during that process. *HELP! for Parents of Children from Ages Six to Twelve Years* helps us as parents see that our children are like other children this age and that other parents have the same problems we do. By offering us alternative ways of looking at the situations we face as parents, it shows us how to stay out of power struggles with our children. It reinforces the importance of having a few—not eighty-five —firm, but not rigid, rules, and it gives us, as adults, support for being in charge of the rules and for improving our own ways of caring for ourselves and others. This is a support group in a book.

—Carol Gesme,
Creator of the *Ups and Downs with Feelings* game

What Is This Book About?

This is a book written for parents by parents.

It is for the days when you don't know what to do or when what you're doing isn't working. It is *not* a theoretical book about the times when things are going smoothly. It *is* a book of specific, practical suggestions for handling different problems that parents have sought help for in parenting classes around the country.

These parents have participated in groups led by facilitators who are trained in the techniques used in "Self-Esteem: A Family Affair" classes. One of these techniques, called the "Suggestion Circle," is used to collect options for parents with problems. Here's how it works. In class, members sit in a circle and listen to a parent describe a problem. Each member of the Circle then offers his or her best suggestion for dealing with it. In this way, the person with the problem benefits from the collective wisdom and experience of the whole group and goes home with a list of suggestions or options.

The Suggestion Circle process is different from brainstorming, which encourages people to offer every idea that comes to mind. It's also different from listening to the teacher or the expert provide "the correct answer." In a Suggestion Circle, *every* answer comes from an "authority," a parent, day-care provider, uncle, aunt, or grandparent. And every answer is "correct," since it worked for the person who discovered it—sometimes after many years of experience. The resulting list provides a variety of suggestions and encourages flexibility in the listener or reader. It may suggest a new way of perceiving the problem.

We chose these eighty-one Circles because they represent problems that we hear about repeatedly in classes or that seem particularly difficult for parents. Facilitators collected the suggestions and asked the parents if we could share their responses with you in these books. Each Circle includes the name of the first facilitator who sent the problem to us and the location of the class or group. Since similar problems come up in different parts of the country, we have combined suggestions from more than one group.

You will notice that often the suggestions contradict one another. That needn't bother you. Parents and children and homes are different, and what works with one may not work with another or at another time. Use what works for you!

You will find the Suggestion Circles grouped in clusters according to subject matter. We have eliminated any ideas that advocated violence, both because child abuse is illegal and because we do not believe violence helps children. We have also eliminated suggestions that implied that parents or children are helpless or that a problem was not serious. We assume that if parents ask for help, the problems are important and serious to them.

In the opening pages of the book, we have outlined the characteristic tasks of this stage of development and described how parents may abuse children if they misunderstand those tasks. We have also given short explanations of *affirmations*, *recycling*, and other topics that are important parts of the "Self-Esteem: A Family Affair" class and that are referred to in the Circles.

So here they are, some short reference pieces and eighty-one Circles, eighty-one collections of the best ideas from parents who have been there, to you who are there now.

—The Editors

How to Use This Book

You can use this book to help you think. When you want ideas about how to solve a problem, look in the table of contents for a cluster title that seems to include your problem. For example, for the problem of children arguing with each other, look under "Brothers and Sisters, Friends and Peers." Or look in the index for words that describe your problem (like *arguing, name-calling, sibling rivalry,* or *competition*), and read about the problems that sound most like yours.

Reading about what other parents have done will remind you that there are many ways to solve problems and that you can find and try out new ways that work for you and your child. If you read a list over several times, you will probably find ideas you missed the first time. Some of the suggestions may not fit your situation or your parenting style, and some of the lists contain contradictions, since there are lots of ways to raise children. Think about which suggestions sound useful for your particular problem.

Our purpose is not to give "one right answer" but to support and stimulate your thinking by offering the wisdom of hundreds of the real child-rearing experts—parents themselves.

Remember that these suggestions are *not* listed in an order of importance. They were offered by a circle of people. If we had printed them in circles, this would be a very big book! We offer them in vertical lists to make a small and convenient book, not to imply that the top suggestion is best.

Use the short sections at the beginning and ending of the book as you need them. For a picture of normal six- to twelve-year-old behavior, read **Ages and Stages** and **About Abuse**. You can use that information to think about whether your expectations are reasonable.

The **Affirmations for Growth** section is about healthy messages or beliefs that children this age need to decide are true for them. Look at **Structuring for Success** for ways to foster responsibility in children. The section called **Parents Get Another Chance—Recycling** reminds us that our own growth never stops and that we, too, are doing our own developmental tasks.

If you are distressed about how anger is expressed inappropriately or repressed at your house, consider using a **Fuss Box**. There are also directions to follow if you want to run your own **Suggestion Circle** and ideas about where to go for additional support.

So read and think. Honor yourself for the many things you do well with your children. Celebrate your growth and the growth of your children. Change when you need to. Remember that your parents did the best they could. You are doing the best you can. If you want to learn some new ways of parenting, it is never too late to start.

Note: Throughout this book, we have alternated masculine and feminine pronouns; in one section or Circle, the child will be a "she," in the next a "he." In each case, please read "all children."

—Jean Illsley Clarke

Ages and Stages

The job of six- to twelve-year-old children is to learn many skills and how to do things well their own way. To achieve this, they practice skills and explore rules. They consider what rules are, how they are made, and how they can be broken. In addition, they think about what values and morals are and how their values and morals contribute to who they are. This exploration of rules and values enables them to learn how to take care of themselves and how to guide their lives.

How do they do this?

- *They ask questions.* The information they gather helps them do things their own way.
- *They practice.* They engage in a wide variety of activities, and they willingly practice over and over the skills in which they're interested.
- *They compare.* They may say, "At Sally's house they do it this way. At Tommy's house they get to stay up until ten. Why can't I? Ann has designer jeans. When do I get mine?"
- *They test.* They test their parents' rules to the nth degree. They need to determine which rules are firm and which can be broken.
- *They disagree.* They need to know that they can disagree and still be loved. Disagreeing helps them form their own opinions. Learning to disagree in an accepting, safe setting will enable them to be assertive and not to yield to peer pressure. A healthy argument or debate shows them that children and adults are entitled to

6

their own opinions, thoughts, and feelings. Parents' willingness to engage in a healthy argument or debate reinforces the belief that children are entitled to their own opinions.

The job of the parent is
- To give unconditional love.
- To expose children to a wide variety of opportunities.
- To give accurate information.
- To give them the chance to explore different skills.
- To maintain the necessary structure for success, including rules.
- To expect the six- to twelve-year-old to challenge those rules. The parent must be prepared to explain, defend, and examine the rules. The parent must know which rules are negotiable and which are not negotiable.

To enable the child to test rules, the parents must create a protective and nurturing environment. In this environment, they will listen to the child's story, problem, or opinion. They will expect him to think and to separate fantasy from reality. The parents will explain their values to the child. This explanation of skills, rules, and values will help the child to know why a rule is needed. The child also needs affirmations that he is expected to think clearly, to solve problems, and to argue. Some children who are busy learning and exploring rules are warm, open, and affectionate. Others seem quite self-contained, while others are downright cantankerous.

This explaining, defending, and challenging of rules may tax the energy of the most enthusiastic parent. In order to maintain enthusiasm and powerful parenting, parents must take good care of themselves. They must be sure that they are getting their own needs met, and are modeling lives filled with supportive structures and functional rules. Parenting a six- to twelve-year-old also gives parents the opportunity to examine their own rules for living and to change the rules that do not work.

—Sandra Sittko and Deane Gradous

Structuring for Success

One of the ways in which parents can help their children become successful is to teach them how to structure. What is structure? It is all of the ways people organize activities. Structuring for success includes all the big and little things that people do to assure positive outcomes. Children learn how to structure from experiencing it and from observation and direct teaching.

For example, how do children learn to manage money?

- By having fifty cents, or five or ten dollars of their own to spend or save.
- By hassling with adults about what is worth buying.
- By making purchasing mistakes with five dollars now, rather than $1,000 later.
- By earning money.

Most lifetime skills are learned in the same way — in small bits. You cannot learn how to earn a living all at once, but you can learn how to do many small tasks productively.

Parenting the six- to twelve-year-old child presents a special opportunity for parents to model the ways they build their own structures. Children need to observe how adults organize for a task, learn new skills, stick to a job, plan a picnic, and so on through all the many skills adults use to do things successfully.

During this stage, children are building their own structures: how to get to school on time, do their homework, follow the rules, enjoy learning, and make new friends. They learn by *doing* these things. They need the support of parents and teachers who care enough to show children how to try new experiences and how to do old things more skillfully, who insist that homework be done, and who encourage responsibility by negotiating flexible rules and enforcing those rules that are firm. Parents allow children to experience the natural consequences of their behavior (unless the children will be unsafe), or parents set logical consequences and carry through with them, starting with small penalties or rewards and increasing them if needed.

The steps for learning structures are important for parents to use and teach to children.
• Define the goal.
• Divide the task into small pieces.
• Practice one piece at a time.
• Visualize knowing how and doing well.
• Decide when the task is finished.
• Use mistakes as learning tools for change.
• Reward or celebrate small and large successes.
• Offer permission to succeed and to work easily.

Every new skill that children learn helps raise their self-esteem. Parents facilitate their children's success in school and society by making and enforcing rules and by teaching responsibilities, new learnings, and skill building—by structuring for success. These things are worth doing.

—Deane Gradous

About Abuse

Child abuse and neglect are prevalent and perhaps epidemic in our society today. We feel strongly that all children are to be valued and cherished. We believe that children will be better protected when parents know the causes and signs of child abuse and when they learn ways to keep children safe.

Causes of Child Abuse

There are many causes of child abuse. Since this is not a book about the ills of society or emotionally disturbed individuals but about normal, healthy parents and children, we will address only the abuse that springs from parents' misunderstanding of normal growth and development of children at different ages. Sometimes, as children go about their developmental tasks, they do things that are misinterpreted by adults who then may be overly severe or hurtful in an attempt to stop or control those normal behaviors. Parents may believe that they are "disciplining," but when they punish their children for doing what is developmentally correct and normal, children are hurt physically or emotionally.

The following behaviors of children this age are frequently misunderstood:

- School-age children are deciding about their own rules. They question all rules, including those of their parents. Many caring adults misinterpret this as "mouthing off." Parents can be firm on a few important rules and spend time with the kids negotiating others.

- Children this age are using rational thinking and show signs of adult thinking. Adults sometimes seize on this sign of new thinking as an opportunity to push children with a "hurry-up-and-grow-up-fast" message. It is important to let children be children.
- Six- to twelve-year-old children are beginning to develop secondary sexual characteristics. Unfortunately, the media and others in our society often offer the fantasy that these children are highly desirable sexually. Any sexual touching of children by adults is abuse.

Signs of Child Abuse

Here are some physical signs that may indicate abuse of a child this age:

- Any unusual marks, particularly around the upper thighs, genitalia, or anus.
- Straight-line bruises that may come from a ruler or belt.
- Significant change in school performance.
- Behavior problems such as drug abuse, soiling, stealing, fire-starting, or eating disorders.
- Signs of depression.

Keeping Children Safe

You keep your children safe when you

- Remember that children need some clear rules (for example, about bedtime on school nights, chores, etc.) and they need to have those rules enforced.

- Make certain your children are capable of staying alone before leaving them alone. Pay special attention to their ability to follow safety rules.
- See that children use seat belts on all car trips— short or long.
- Become aware of the extent of alcohol abuse and drug abuse in your child's environment and take action to protect your child from that abuse. Refuse to serve your children alcoholic beverages. The chances of alcohol causing liver damage in a child this age are much greater than in an adult.
- Establish yourself as a reliable source of information about people, the world, and sex. Explain about sexual growth to your children caringly, lovingly, and knowledgeably, or get a specially trained adult to do it. Tell children that washroom walls or people in back halls offer inaccurate or incomplete information about sex. It is important for children this age to receive lots of nurturing touch, but they should *never* be touched sexually by adults. Tell them to report sexual touches or sexual invitations by adults or teenagers to you.

If you suspect abuse of any kind, find a way to protect your child. Get help if you need it. Report the abuser to the child protection service in your area. See **Where to Go for Additional Support**.

—Christine Ternand, M.D.

Affirmations for Growth

At each period or stage of growth in children's lives there are certain tasks they need to master and certain decisions they need to make if they are to grow into loving, capable, responsible adults.

Parents can help children master these tasks by providing safe, structured, stimulating environments and experiences. Parents can encourage their children to make appropriate decisions by challenging inappropriate behavior and by giving their children affirmations.

What are affirmations? Affirmations are all the things we do or say that imply that children are lovable and capable. We affirm children with our words and our actions, our body language, our facial expressions, and our tone of voice.

Here are some special affirming messages that will help children in this stage of growth (ages six through twelve), when they are developing their own structures, competence, and values, and are learning about the relevance of rules.

Affirmations for Structure

- You can think before you say yes or no and learn from your mistakes.
- You can trust your intuition to help you decide what to do.
- You can find a way of doing things that works for you.

- You can learn the rules that help you live with others.
- You can learn when and how to disagree.
- You can think for yourself and get help instead of staying in distress.
- I love you even when we differ; I love growing with you.

You give these affirmations by the way you interact with your children, challenge their thinking, and encourage them to test values, examine rules, acquire information and skills, and experience consequences.

In addition to all the things you do, you can *say* these affirmations directly in supportive, loving ways.

Belief in these affirmations helps children achieve independence and encourages them to develop strong, internal self-responsibility. The affirmations are powerful antidotes to peer pressure. Giving them may take effort, especially on days when the children are hassling you and pushing the limits to find out what rules are firm and important and what happens when rules are broken.

Of course, you have to believe these messages yourself, or they become confusing or crazy double messages. If you don't understand or believe an affirmation, don't give that one until you do believe it.

Once human beings have entered each developmental stage, they need to receive the affirmations from that stage for the rest of their lives, so children continue to need the affirmations from earlier stages. Those messages support their

Being, their Doing, their Thinking, and their Identity.

The messages about Being reinforce our right to exist and have needs, to be loved and cared for.

Affirmations for Being

• I'm glad you are alive.
• You belong here.
• What you need is important to me.
• I'm glad you are you.
• You can grow at your own pace.
• You can feel all of your feelings.
• I love you, and I care for you willingly.

The Doing messages focus on the need to reach out and to explore, to initiate, and to be creative.

Affirmations for Doing

• You can explore and experiment, and I will support and protect you.
• You can use all of your senses when you explore.
• You can do things as many times as you need to.
• You can know what you know.
• You can be interested in everything.
• I like to watch you initiate and grow and learn.
• I love you when you are active and when you are quiet.

The Thinking messages support separation and independence.

Affirmations for Thinking

• I'm glad you are starting to think for yourself.
• It's OK for you to be angry, and I won't let you hurt yourself or others.

- You can say no and push and test limits as much as you need to.
- You can learn to think for yourself, and I will think for myself.
- You can think and feel at the same time.
- You can know what you need and ask for help.
- You can become separate from me, and I will continue to love you.

Messages for Identity focus on independence, self-image, and power to support independent thinking.

Affirmations for Identity and Power

- You can explore who you are and find out who other people are.
- You can be powerful and ask for help at the same time.
- You can try out different roles and ways of being powerful.
- You can find out the results of your behavior.
- All of your feelings are OK with me.
- You can learn what is pretend and what is real.
- I love who you are.

If you believe, from observing your child's attitude or behavior, that your child did not "get" some of these affirmations during younger years, focus on those affirmations now. You can refer to earlier *HELP!* books for additional readings about each stage. Remember, it is never too late for you to start believing and offering the affirmations.

You can read more about what affirmations mean and don't mean and how to use them in families in Clarke's *Self-Esteem: A Family*

Affair. These affirmations are adapted from Pamela Levin's *Becoming the Way We Are*. (See **Resources**.)

When you discover additional affirmations that your child needs, write them in your book and give them to your child.

—Jean Illsley Clarke

Parents Get Another Chance—
Recycling

When children are increasing their skills and challenging the rules, parents sometimes begin to chafe at the rules in their own lives and decide to learn new skills, too.

One of the benefits of caring for six- to twelve-year-old children is that parents can use that time to rework or recycle their own internal values and structures and the how and why of the things they do.

What Is Recycling?

Recycling is the name given to the rhythmic, cyclical growth process that individuals go through, often without noticing it, in which they learn to do important developmental tasks in ever more competent and sophisticated ways. Pamela Levin discusses the theory in *Becoming the Way We Are*. Recycling does not mean that we adults regress to a childlike state, but rather that our life experiences demand that we continually recreate or develop more skillful ways of doing old life-supporting tasks while we are doing new adult stage tasks. Besides having a natural rhythm for our adult tasks, we as parents are often triggered to recycle whatever stages our children are in. I have talked with hundreds of parents about this idea. Many of them have reported, often with some surprise, that they *are* working on some of the same tasks as their children. It is a normal, healthy, and hopeful aspect of living with growing children.

Recycling the Tasks of Internalizing Our Own Values and Structures

While the children are busy learning new skills and exploring the importance of rules, parents are busy learning, too. They learn new skills to help their children, to support their own career advancement, or for sheer enjoyment. Parents who are pushed by children of this age to enforce and defend family rules can take this opportunity to reevaluate personal and family rules, to drop dysfunctional ones, to change and update others, and to strengthen important, basic values.

Parents who did not learn the skills of hassling during their own childhood can practice that assertive skill now as they learn to challenge their children to think clearly. Parents can learn to handle the hassling in a good-natured way that keeps it enjoyable for the parent and challenges the child to think.

The affirmations that are helpful to our children are also healthy for us. (See page 14.) Because many of us never received or decided not to believe some of those healthy messages (or only believe them partly), this is an ideal time to accept those messages for ourselves and to claim more of our ability to be whole, healthy, joyful adults. If you didn't get the affirmations you needed the first time around, you can take them now as you offer them to your children.

—Jean Illsley Clarke

A. Rules, Responsibility, and Money

I plan to limit my children's TV watching. Can someone help me make the rules so it will be easier for me and my children to stick to them?

- Set up a system. Have a reward for keeping to the new schedule you set together.
- Spell out which programs are acceptable and ask your children to pick a certain number from within that group.
- Hold a family meeting. Discuss everyone's wants and needs and set family TV rules. Read Dreikurs' *Family Council*. (See **Resources**.)
- Together, select programs to watch for the week and circle them in the TV schedule.
- Give each child a certain number of quarters for the week. Have the child pay for each program watched. If all the money isn't used, the child may spend it as she wishes. Or use marbles.
- Set a family rule that school work must be done and homework completed before TV watching and hold everybody to it.
- On Sunday morning with the family, identify informational and entertaining shows allowed for the week. Limit TV watching to those.
- Together, decide ahead of time how conflicts over who picks the show will be resolved.
- Post the rules on the refrigerator.

Thanks to Christine Ternand, Circle from St. Paul, Minnesota

How can I know how much housework to expect of my child?

• Check out his age and ability (can he do the task, or can he learn how?) when determining what tasks to assign.

• Start by expecting him to take care of his own possessions and room. Give him small household chores and reward him for their completion. Say, "We all share in the family work. Thank you."

• Hold a family council so that the family can decide together how much will be expected of each member. See Dreikurs' *Family Council.* (See **Resources**.)

• Have a job list. The child chooses several small jobs or one big job.

• Certainly kids six and over should do the daily care of their own rooms and help with total household care. Ten-year-olds can do almost any chore (but slavery is illegal).

• Assign tasks according to age and ability, and stick to the expectation that the tasks will be done. They will need this ability to finish things later in life when they do things on their own.

(See also A-5, A-8, C-5, C-7.)

Thanks to Barbara Morgan, Circle from Seattle, Washington

I have a twelve-year-old daughter who is behaving irresponsibly. How can I help her be more responsible?

- Show her how to do things and expect her to do them well.
- Remind her often that you love her, and tell her when you notice her doing something well.
- When you are angry about something she hasn't done, tell her and then insist that she do it.
- Be clear about your expectations.
- When she thinks clearly, compliment her thinking.
- Remember: What you stroke is what you get. If she only gets attention when she messes up, she will probably continue to mess up.
- Sit down with her, and the two of you write a list of agreed-upon rules. Decide together on rewards when she keeps the rules and consequences when she breaks them.
- Let her experience the logical consequences of her behavior—replace her lost gloves with a less expensive pair and have her pay for the new pair.
- Make sure she knows what you consider irresponsible behavior and what its results are.
- The Eyre book, *Teaching Children Responsibility*, describes many different ways of helping children become responsible. (See **Resources.**)

(See also B-1, B-8, and **Structure for Success**.)

Thanks to Marilyn Sackariason, Circle from Minneapolis, Minnesota

When I start to play a game with my eight-year-old son, he hassles over the rules and generally ruins the fun. What can I do?

- Do some other activity with him instead of playing that game.
- Tell him he's fun to be with when he *is* fun to be with.
- Turn the hassling into fun, enjoy it, and learn how to hassle playfully yourself.
- Stop playing when it becomes unpleasant.
- Ask him if he wants an arbitrator to decide on the rules.
- Hassle with him only as long as you and he can enjoy each other.
- Remember that hassling is one way to learn about rules.
- Sometimes let him establish rules, and you follow them, too.
- Reread the rules on the game box or consult *Hoyle's Card Games*. (See **Resources**.)
- Create your own game with him, and write down the rules.
- Change your own attitude by visualizing him playing happily and peacefully.
- Breathe deeply and think about what you and he want to accomplish with this time together.
- Give him positive feedback when he follows rules.

Thanks to Nancy Drake, Circle from Walnut Creek, California

My child wants to be paid for everything she does around the house. What can I do?

- Children are a part of the family and deserve some of the family resources.
- "Pay" her in some other form, such as a toy, a new piece of clothing, or a trip to the zoo.
- Explain that you all work together in your family and that everyone does certain household tasks without payment.
- Agree on the chores she will be paid for. Don't pay her if she doesn't do the chore.
- Kids should do household chores, and if we have enough money to pay, then we do.
- Remember, earning your own money is important.
- Don't pay. Give her an allowance not connected to helping around the house.
- Pay her for some chores and not for others.

(See also A-2, A-3, A-8.)

Thanks to Darlene Montz, Circle from Yakima, Washington

My kids mow lawns and babysit. Who decides what they do with the money?

- They do.
- Contract with them to save half and spend half.
- Treat all family income as belonging to the family—kids' income too. They add to the family pot and take it out according to need.
- Show them how to budget by budgeting for family expenses and expecting them to contribute to saving for some important family purchase.
- It's OK to insist that they use a portion of their earnings to support their needs for clothing, food, school supplies, and so on.
- Remember that they will learn from making purchasing mistakes with their own money, especially if they can talk it over with you.

Thanks to Judy Popp, Circle from Yakima, Washington

My eight-year-old son doesn't get ready on time in the morning. What can I do?

- You schedule the morning routine and walk him through it a few times to be sure he knows what he needs to do.
- Discuss with him why he is not getting ready. He may not want to go to school. Find out why.
- The night before, tell him that you love him and will look forward to seeing him in the morning.
- Teach him how to set a timer or the clock radio so it will go on at the time he should be *finished* dressing.
- Call him only once. Let him be late and take the consequences: walk to school or miss the day of school with no TV.
- Have him do more of his getting ready at night.
- Send him to bed a half-hour earlier each week until he gets enough sleep to wake easily in the morning.
- Wake him with a back rub.
- Establish rewards for getting up on time.
- Plan to do something together the first ten minutes of the morning. Read a book together, exercise, make pancakes.

(See also B-9, D-2, D-5, D-7.)

Thanks to Barb Kobe, Circle from Crystal, Minnesota

My daughter will not clean her room. What can I do?

- Take away a privilege. Having one's own room is a privilege in some families.
- Offer instruction on room cleaning and how to break the task into little steps—bedmaking, picking up clothing, etc.
- Close the door.
- Some things are more fun with help. You could team up and share jobs around the house.
- Let her have a "messy corner" in her room. The rest of the room is to be neat.
- Reward her when she keeps her room clean several days in a row.
- Tell her that she is a good housekeeper whenever she demonstrates this skill.
- With your daughter, draw up a plan for redecorating the room later and for making it look a little nicer now.
- Tell her that you will clean her room if she will clean the living room.
- Give her an "I will clean your room one time" certificate. She may discover that she likes a clean room.

(See also A-2, A-5.)

Thanks to Nancy O'Hara, Circle from Minneapolis, Minnesota

At what age can my older child be expected to "babysit" our younger ones or the neighbor's kids, and how can I help him be successful?

- Our kids started babysitting at ten or eleven. That's a fairly common age for this.
- Let him know you are available to answer questions or to help in an emergency.
- Help him with suggestions and by example. Show him how by visiting him when he's babysitting the first couple of times.
- Make a list with him of "important rules for babysitting" such as this one:
  1. No phone calls
  2. No visitors
  3. This is a job; treat it like one. Get phone numbers and parental direction
  4. Follow safety guideline
- Ten is too young to babysit. You can help him out by not allowing it.
- Send him to a babysitting clinic.
- Ask him to listen to Clarke's tapes on child development, *The Wonderful Busy Ones* and *The Terrific Twos*, and tell you what he heard about good care for each age child. (See **Resources**.)
- Let him start being "the sitter" for the younger ones in your home for a half-hour while you are home to answer questions. Set the timer. As soon as he starts to learn the rules, start to pay him.

Thanks to Kathy Bliven Huseby, Circle from Minneapolis, Minnesota

B. Discipline

What is the difference between discipline and punishment?

- Discipline says, "Stop. Do something else instead." Punishment says, "You did something wrong and you are bad!"
- Discipline sets the child up for success next time. Punishment focuses on failure.
- If there is physical hurt, it is punishment.
- Discipline is something that shows consequences, but is not as severe as punishment.
- Discipline does not expect more than a child this age can do. Punishment often does.
- Discipline is learning the right and wrong of life. Punishment is the negative side of discipline.
- Discipline addresses the *act* as wrong. Punishment addresses the *person* as wrong.
- Discipline has a good chance of being effective. The results of punishment are unpredictable.
- Discipline comes from thought, and punishment comes from anger.
- Punishment is being disciplined without knowing what's expected of you.
- If the parent feels gleeful or vengeful, it's punishment.

(See also B-10, I-15.)

Thanks to Christine Ternand, Circle from St. Paul, Minnesota

What can I do instead of hitting, yelling, or verbally abusing my children?

• Get professional counseling.
• Leave the room. Later talk to the child about why you were angry.
• Take a parenting class.
• Count to twenty.
• Use a Fuss Box. (See page 120.)
• Tell your angry thoughts to a tape recorder and play it back. What did you hear?
• Close your eyes and think about the positive qualities of the child; then share your positive thoughts with that child.
• Hit a pillow, if that is what you tell your children to do when they are angry.
• Be aware of why you are angry, breathe deeply, and think.
• Tell the child that you are angry, why you are angry, and calmly discuss what to do about it.
• Call your local crisis hot-line.

(See also A-3, B-1, B-10, I-15.)

Thanks to Deane Gradous, Circle from St. Paul, Minnesota

What do I do when my child says, "I won't, and you can't make me"?

- Offer options instead of ultimatums.
- Make it clear which rules are bendable and which she has to follow.
- Give the kid some consequences.
- Establish parent and child roles; and make sure your child knows you are in charge.
- Say, "Look, that's the way I felt about grocery shopping this week, but I did it anyway. People have to do some things they don't like."
- Say, "I hear you say 'I won't'; what do you say 'I will' to?"
- Acknowledge her saying a loud and strong "no." Remember, this is what we want her to say when someone offers her drugs.
- When it's a non-negotiable rule say, "Are you going to do it yourself, or am I going to help you?"
- Maybe the child is saying "Listen to me—I want to be heard!"
- Check out your language or your tone of voice. Maybe you asked her to do the thing in a way that assumed she would be rebellious.
- Don't say, "Will you . . . ?" unless "no" is an OK response. If you want her to do something, tell her to do it; don't ask.

(See also E-6.)

Thanks to Deane Gradous, Circle from St. Paul, Minnesota

My child is using lots of dirty words, and I disapprove. What can I do?

• Check your feelings as to why the words are "hot."

• Ask him to use nonsense words instead.

• Tell the child how bad you feel being around such language.

• Don't make a big fuss over this as it adds importance to the words. Also, don't use them yourself.

• Calmly state you don't like to hear those words and suggest he go into his room to say them so you don't have to hear them.

• Point out your disapproval of this language to him initially, and then ignore it. It may be just a way of getting a reaction from you. If the problem continues, ask him if he has a reason for using words you don't like.

• Say, "If you use those words around me, I will expect you to. . . ." Then set a consequence you can live with, such as having your child list four ways he could have said that without dirty words.

• Tell him about family values and expect him to respect them.

• Totally ignore the words for one month and see if he stops using them.

(See also B-8, E-4.)

Thanks to Darlene Montz, Circle from Yakima, Washington

My children, ages five and seven, ride their bikes in the street. It is not safe. What can I do?

• Tell them why you are concerned, and tell them where they *can* ride.
• If your local police offer classes, take them to a class on bike safety.
• Go over safety rules about how and when to ride in the street.
• Set definite rules and take the bikes away for one day the first time a rule is broken, two days the second time, etc.
• Go riding with them to teach them safety rules for riding in streets. Then go with them sometimes to see if they are obeying the rules.
• Have the whole family ride on the bike paths in parks.
• While you show them how to maintain and clean their bikes in order to help them understand the value of the bikes, talk with them about safety rules and the value of their bodies.

(See also A-3, B-1.)

Thanks to Bernice Brotherton, Circle from St. Paul, Minnesota

I want suggestions for ways to help my son, age seven, to be a better listener when I ask him to do something or give him directions.

• Touch his arm or hand to get his attention before you talk to him.
• Make sure you have eye contact.
• Sometimes talk to him at his eye level.
• Try drawing pictures to remind him or writing the directions in words he can read.
• Ask him to repeat back to you what you just told him. If that doesn't work, ask him what he felt or saw in his mind's eye.
• Reward him when he follows directions.
• At the end of the day, during his quiet time before bed, tell him some of the ways you saw him being a good listener.
• Have the doctor check his hearing. Remember, when he has a cold or sinus infection, his hearing may be temporarily impaired.
• Affirm his listening well when you notice him doing it.
• Seven-year-olds are more interested in doing than in listening to directions. Sometimes it will be OK to let him go ahead without direction and to learn from that.
• Let him look away or ask him if he wants you to write out the task.

(See also E-8, I-2.)

Thanks to Nat Houtz, Circle from Seattle, Washington

My kids snack a lot, and then they aren't hungry at mealtime. I want them to eat meals at the table. How do other families handle this problem?

• Set clear times about when they can and can't snack.
• Try having dinner earlier.
• Don't buy junk food. Keep fresh cleaned vegetables in the refrigerator. Snacking on them will do less harm to their appetites at mealtime.
• Serve apples and make a rule as to the latest time they can eat them.
• Help them plan a game or fun activity to do before mealtime so that they don't snack out of boredom.
• Consider serving five small meals a day instead of three large ones.
• Work out a list of foods acceptable for snacks and buy only those.
• Have a family conference to discuss how to resolve the problem.
• Hold a family Suggestion Circle. (See page 125.)
• Have the kids help plan the menus. Have them help cook the meals.

(See also H-1.)

Thanks to Kitty Lindall, Circle from Prior Lake, Minnesota

My son's best friend won't follow our house rules. What shall I do?

• Confront the friend. List your important house rules for him and tell him that everyone in your house follows these rules.

• Explain the rules again. Then tell him that if he does not obey your house rules, he will be sent home and cannot return until the next day. Follow through with this.

• Be clear about the rules so that both your son and the friend know the rules. If you like the friend, let him know that you do.

• In a friendly way, explain that your house rules may be different from his. Tell him that you expect him to follow your rules at your house.

• Post the rules.

• Say, "Good job!" when the friend follows a rule.

• Use this opportunity to evaluate your house rules and see if they are reasonable.

• Let your son know you expect him to be part of the solution.

• Kids who follow the rules get jelly beans.

Thanks to Mary Paananen, Circle from Seattle, Washington

How can I get my kids, ages five and seven, to bed on time?

- Start "ready-for-bed" time early enough so they can read by themselves or play with a toy for fifteen minutes before lights out.
- Half an hour before bedtime ring a signal bell.
- Set a timer for bedtime. When the bell goes off, they are to turn it off and go to bed.
- Tell them you need some time for yourself.
- Don't give chocolate or other caffeinated or sweet foods in the evening.
- Explain about sleep and its benefits. Discuss how many hours are needed.
- Spend some time with each child just before bed.
- Routine is important; be consistent.
- Quiet time is important. Read or talk; don't roughhouse, tease, or tickle just before bed.
- Have them spend ten to thirty minutes before bedtime doing a special project for themselves.
- Make a game of "Everyone who's in bed in five minutes wins." Then firmly put anyone back in bed who gets up.
- Put a paper clock next to the real clock, and when the hands match, it is time for bed.

Thanks to Evelyn Goodall, Circle from Calgary, Alberta, Canada

What can I do when I realize that I am doing things to my kids that my parents did to me and I vowed I would never do?

- Notice all the ways in which you are copying your parents. Keep the ones that are positive. Change only those that are not positive.
- If you are doing something that you hated as a child but now realize is necessary, accept it. I have told my kids, "Wow, I sound just like my mother. How do you like that? I used to hate it when she said that! But it is important!"
- Count to ten or say the ABCs. Then apologize and think of a better way.
- Get therapy.
- Apologize to your children when you have used an old negative method. Talk about how you will handle such a situation next time.
- Tell your kids what your parents did well and ask your kids to tell you what you do well.
- Take a parenting class. Try out new ways of disciplining every week until you find ways that you like.
- Write down a list of alternative ways to discipline. Then, consult your list before disciplining.
- Study Elizabeth Crary's book, *Without Spanking or Spoiling*. (See **Resources**.)

(See also B-2.)

Thanks to Sandra Sittko, Circle from St. Paul, Minnesota

C. Brothers and Sisters, Friends and Peers

My child is putting down younger children in the family and bossing them. What should a parent do?

- Say, "I don't like what you are saying. Please say something positive or leave the room."
- Hold up a *stop* sign.
- Make a "No Put-Down" rule. Post it and insist the whole family observe it.
- Read Claude Steiner's *Warm Fuzzy Tale* to all of them. (See **Resources**.)
- Send her for a *time out*.
- Put your arm around her. Say in a pleasant tone, "In this family we don't put each other down. We help each other. How can I help you?"
- Show her the affirmations. Ask her which of those she'd rather tell her siblings. (See page 14.)
- Offer love to *all* the children.
- Teach the children to *fall down* when they hear a *put down*. It is hard to continue put downs when everyone else is lying on the floor playing dead.
- Ask her to teach them instead of bossing them.
- When the older one is to be in charge, tell the younger ones how long it will last.
- When giving the older one the responsibility of watching the younger ones, give her guidelines and explain how to do it with skill.
- Send her to babysitting school.

(See also G-2.)

Thanks to Judi Salts, Circle from Yakima, Washington

What can I do when my six- and eight-year-olds tattle on each other?

• Ask the librarian to find some books about tattling. Read the stories before bedtime or ask the children to read them when you are together in the car.

• Sit down with them and explain the difference between tattling and reporting, which is giving you important information that you should have.

• When the tattling is about a health or safety issue, listen.

• Tell them they can tattle into a tape recorder if they need to tattle. They can erase the tape when they want to listen to something that's more fun.

• Tell the children you want to hear both sides.

• Clap your hands over your ears.

• Give each child lots of attention when he or she is not tattling. This behavior may be a bid for attention.

• Tell the children that they have a problem and they can decide what to do about it.

• You could get another adult to play-act tattling in front of the children. Say, "This is tattling and I won't listen to it."

(See also E-5.)

Thanks to Melanie Weiss, Circle from Bellevue, Washington

My daughter complains that she is tired of sharing a bedroom with her younger sister. She wants her own room.

• Say, "You could have the guest room, but then you'd have to move out every time we have company or when exchange students come."
• Remodel the basement and include another bedroom in your plan.
• Place a desk, chest of drawers, or bookcase to divide the room.
• Ask, "What do you suggest? Do you have a better way of arranging the bedrooms we have?"
• Suggest that they arrange to spend an hour alone in the bedroom each day for private time.
• Give the older sister a "special" nook in another part of the house.
• Find out what the problem is. A need for privacy? Time alone? Safety of person? Personal belongings? No place for friends? Then decide what to do.

Thanks to Rosemary and Cy Rief, Circle from Yakima, Washington

My seven- and nine-year-olds are too competitive. What can I do to downplay the competition?

- Plan activities for them that take cooperation between two people.
- Look for differences in each child to praise and affirm. Get them to compete in separate areas.
- Buy Rhea Zakich's "The Ungame" and play it with your family. (See **Resources**.)
- Stress each child's individuality and avoid trying to make things fair and equal. Spend some time alone with each of them.
- Check out how you and your spouse are relating in front of them. Do you cooperate or do you compete?
- Get the *New Games Book* by Andrew Fluegelman and use it. (See **Resources**.)
- Get the whole family involved in a cooperative venture and talk about the importance of working together.
- Don't compare them. Say, "You do that well!" Do not say, "You do that better than your sister."
- Give some privileges and responsibilities to the nine-year-old that the other has to wait until age nine for.
- Read *Kids Can Cooperate*, by Elizabeth Crary, and *Raising Brothers and Sisters Without Raising the Roof*, by Andrew and Carole Calladine. (See **Resources**.)

Thanks to Jean Clarke, Circle from Plymouth, Minnesota

**What can I do when my son and daughter ask,
"Why do _I_ have to do the dishes?" In other words,
why not the other one?**

• Change the chore list every week.
• Say, "You must do the dishes now. We will talk
  about family chores later this evening."
• Ask, "What do you think you could do about
  this problem?" Listen well. They might have a
  better idea.
• Center your body and say, "You know whose
  responsibility the dishes are this week."
• Suggest that they trade chores with each other.
  Remind them that their jobs must be done, no
  matter who does them.
• Sometimes when all the chores are finished
  quickly and well, do a special family activity.

(See also A-2, A-8.)

Thanks to Kitty Lindall, Circle from Shakopee,
Minnesota

My kids fight a lot. What can I do?

- Say, "I'm not interested in listening to you fight. Please leave the area."
- Set a rule that arguments are to be sung. My kids ended up laughing before many minutes were up.
- Stop them. Clarify your rules about name-calling and hitting. Determine consequences and then follow through.
- Whisper, "I love you" in the ear of each child, and kiss each one.
- If they are harming one another physically, stop them.
- Separate them. Invite them to write down what they think the fight is about. Invite them to come together and settle the issue.
- Do not mediate. Leave.
- Play often with them with lots of body contact. Give hugs. Perhaps they need to be touched.
- Read *He Hit Me First* by Louise Bates Ames. (See **Resources**.)
- Have a family meeting and ask the children if they need anything from other family members to help them live more peaceably.
- Stop the fight and have them report one thing they value about each other.

(See also C-4, D-4.)

Thanks to Harold Nordeman, Circle from Cincinnati, Ohio

How can I deal with my seven-year-old who wants all the privileges that are given to my ten-year-old?

• Set the rules and privileges for each child, and stick with them.

• Explain about age differences. Go back to when they were one and four. Four could talk, one could not. The seven-year-old does not have all the privileges nor all of the responsibilities the ten-year-old has.

• Give lots of love to both of them. Be careful not to fan the competition. Say, "As you get older you get more responsibilities, and with those come privileges."

• Look at each child as an individual. When a child is capable of a responsibility, let him or her be responsible. Privileges come after responsibilities are handled well.

• Say, "I'm pretty sure you know what privileges and responsibilities are appropriate for each of you. You don't have to like them, and you do have to follow them."

• Worry about safety and development and each child's needs, and don't worry about fair.

• Say, "It may not seem fair, and that's the way it is."

(See also C-4.)

Thanks to Deane Gradous, Circle from Minnetonka, Minnesota

My children insist on wearing designer clothes. Virtually all their friends have the "right" shoes and jeans. These clothes don't fit my pocketbook, and I don't think they are appropriate.

- Have your children become a part of the family discussion about finances.
- Tell the children what you will spend for jeans. Let them make up the difference from their allowances or earnings.
- Read David Elkind's *The Hurried Child* for support in not pushing your children to grow up too fast. (See **Resources**.)
- Have them figure out ways to earn money to buy the clothing they want.
- Tell the children that each can have one designer item a season. Set a price limit and let them choose.
- Have a discussion about values and how we judge others by their clothing.
- Teach them how to shop discount houses and sales.
- Give compliments for their personality and not just for their appearance. Clothing doesn't make the person.
- Send them to a school where all the kids wear uniforms.

(See also A-6, F-1.)

Thanks to Lois White, Circle from Minnetonka, Minnesota

I think my child is in a group at school that isn't good for her. What shall I do?

• Talk to the teacher and other parents and see how they perceive the situation.
• Talk with the child. Stress values. Say, "It's OK to have all kinds of friends, but don't hurt yourself or others."
• Model the behavior you want. What kind of values do you and your friends espouse?
• Try to find out what her values are. If this group is really bad, consider changing schools.
• Encourage her to get involved in a sport.
• Give the affirmations for Structure. (See page 14.)
• Encourage activity in positive groups. You could become a Scout leader or a Sunday school teacher and involve her there.
• Don't condemn her friends before you talk to her and find out something about these friends. You may be wrong.
• Encourage her to invite her friends to a party. See if you can learn what she values in them.

Thanks to Linda Buranen, Circle from Plymouth, Minnesota

What do I do when I tell my eleven-year-old he has done something well and he says, "The kids say you shouldn't brag. Cool kids don't like bragging."

- Tell him, "Feeling good about what you have done is not bragging." Teach him the difference, and keep on praising him.

- Compliments are not bragging, but telling someone you received a compliment could be considered bragging. Tell him to choose when and where to celebrate his wins.

- I would begin by building self-esteem with Being affirmations: "You are neat just because you are you." "I love you." As he becomes comfortable with these messages, he will gradually accept recognition or praise for "doing" well. (See page 16.)

- Say, "If you don't want to tell the kids when you do something well, don't. But tell me and be sure to tell yourself."

- Say, "Keep looking for a friend you can brag with. Some day, somewhere, you will find that person, and then you will have a special friend. It is important to be proud of yourself."

- Have him make a list of ten things that he likes about himself and share it with you or some other trusted adult.

(See also G-1.)

Thanks to Linda Buranen, Circle from Plymouth, Minnesota

Our six-year-old idolizes another boy and wants to do everything and have the same things as his idol. What should a parent say or do?

• Say, "I notice that you have a friend you admire. It's great to have a friend you admire lots."

• Say, "Each of us is different. You are Matt and he is Scott."

• Say, "You can think about what Scott does before you decide to do it." Offer the affirmations for Structure. (See page 14.)

• Value your son's requests on their own merit. Tell him how you decide. Whether or not the other boy has it should not be the deciding factor.

• Make some firm family rules about what people do, and stick with them.

• Talk about some people you admire and why you admire them.

• With him find one thing that he can do like the other boy and one thing that he can do just because he is himself, growing up in his own family.

• Take both boys on an outing and give each positive messages for their uniqueness.

• Be sure that the other boy is a good influence on your son. Otherwise encourage him to look for new friends.

Thanks to Ellen Peterson, Circle from Orinda, California

How can I comfort my child when she feels no one likes her and no one likes to play with her?

- Tell your child that you will take her and a friend someplace fun. Show her different ways to invite friends to do some things. If this doesn't work, try again with another child or several children, but only take them one-on-one so they can talk and get to know each other.
- Give her lots of affirmations for Being. (See page 16.)
- Empathize with her: "Sounds like you are feeling left out." Then listen to her some more.
- Invite her to make bread with you. While you knead, talk about how sometimes your friends want to play with you and sometimes not.
- Challenge her thinking. Ask her to tell you three ways the kids show they like her and three ways they show they don't like her.
- Tell her that you believe she will find ways to solve this problem.
- Say, "Wait until after dinner and call Katy again. Maybe she will be home by then."
- Say, "Go get the cards and we will play a game. Practice with me how to play cards and be a friend."

(See also E-1, G-1, G-2.)

Thanks to Rosemary and Cy Rief, Circle from Yakima, Washington

My daughter won't play with boys because she says they have "boy germs." What can I do?

- Don't fuss about it and allow her to have her own feelings on the matter. Realize that this is a phase.
- Hassle her gently. Say, "They do? What kind?"
- Ask her if she has "girl germs."
- Tell her that she can play with boys when she is ready.
- Ask her what "boy germs" are. Is this some distorted sexual information? If so, find the source.
- Take a look at your own friendships. Do you have friends of the opposite sex?
- Tell her, "I remember when I thought that. Now I think that boys and men are just as valuable and as much fun as girls and women."
- Leave her alone. She'll decide when to have boy playmates. I wouldn't force her to play with boys.
- Explain that boys and girls are both important and let her choose her own friends.
- Encourage her to play with girls. She needs to accept and appreciate her sex before she can accept and appreciate a person of the opposite sex.

Thanks to Sandra Sittko, Circle from St. Paul, Minnesota

D. School

My sixth grader is in a new school, and he is having trouble adjusting. How can I help him?

- Identify more specifically the reason he is having trouble. Make sure you understand the problem before you try to solve it.
- If he is not up with his class in some subject, get a tutor.
- Find out what clubs and after-school activities are available and let him choose one or two to try out.
- Discuss ways to make new friends.
- Schedule fun activities and say it's OK to invite a friend.
- Meet with the teachers and ask them for ideas.
- Meet some of the other parents. When you can, arrange for him to meet new kids outside of the school.
- Take time to listen each night. He might do better if he can talk things out with you.
- Give him three more weeks.
- Purchase *Goodbye, House* by Ann Banks and Nancy Evans and go through it together or separately. Perhaps you and he are grieving the loss of his old friends and school and just need some more time to adjust. (See **Resources**.)

(See also C-12, E-1, G-1.)

Thanks to Nancy Delin, Circle from Chaska, Minnesota

My child has been acting up in school. His name has been "on the board" so many times that the teacher called home to talk to me. What can I do?

- Tell your child that this is not what you expected and ask what you can do to help.
- Tell him that he can make it a good day for himself as he leaves for school each morning.
- Offer him the Power and Identity affirmations. Support his power. (See page 17.)
- Have a conference with the teacher and the child. Offer to help them both get this problem resolved.
- Ask his teacher what he does well. Ask her to write his name on the board for doing that well.
- Does he follow the rules at home? If not, build in consequences. What he learns at home will help him at school.
- Make a contract with the teacher, stating the consequences for not following school rules. Tell him to follow the rules at school.
- Ask him how he feels about having his name on the board and what he plans to do about it.
- Expect him to think before he does things. He can learn to keep himself out of trouble.

(See also G-7.)

Thanks to Toni Drucker, Circle from Lafayette, California

My child won't do her homework. Taking away TV doesn't make any difference.

• Set aside a time of the day when adults and kids do quiet work together at the table. Parents do their work and kids do theirs. If she doesn't have homework, she can read or do other quiet work.

• With her, set homework time and play time and stick to it. Invite her to show you her homework when she is done.

• After school offer her a snack, ask her if she has any assignments, and tell her to do her homework right away.

• Don't bail her out. Homework is the child's responsibility.

• Often homework is no big deal in terms of time needed to finish it. She may, however, need your support in learning to do new things and in how to organize. (See **Structuring for Success**.)

• Change the pattern at home if she gets a lot of attention for *not* doing her homework, or if she only gets help when she's in a crisis. Give her energy and attention when she is doing her work.

(See also D-6, D-7, D-8, G-1.)

Thanks to Margo Tobias, Circle from Orinda, California

Our daughter is coming home from school looking for a fight and often finds one. What can I do to help her?

• Ask her if she needs more time with you or your spouse.
• She may be having school problems. Outline the problem with the teacher and work together with the teacher and your child toward a solution.
• Spend time just with her.
• She may be getting negative attention. Tell her, "I'm getting tired of your behavior. Is there something we can talk about to help you with it?"
• Talk with her about her anger or frustration.
• Is she getting enough sleep and eating right?
• Tell her, "Go to your room and settle down."
• Set aside time when she is not fighting and talk with her about her behavior.
• Ask her if she is tense. Teach her songs and exercises to help her relax.
• Teach her to use the Fuss Box. (See page 120.)
• Refuse to spar with her.

(See also C-6.)

Thanks to Nancy O'Hara, Circle from Minneapolis, Minnesota

My six-year-old daughter is tearful and fearful of a teacher who "taps" kids in class. How can I address this problem at an interview with the teacher?

- Feel confident of your right as a parent and don't stop until you are fully satisfied about the physical and psychological safety of your daughter. Talk with the teacher and then the principal, if necessary.
- Affirm yourself for coping with this problem. Also know that other children may be upset.
- Bring up the issue now—don't put it off.
- It is important to talk with your daughter to find out how she feels. Get more information. Make sure she is telling you specifically what the problem is. Give her support.
- Share with the teacher your concern about having to bring up the subject. Treat the teacher with respect but not reverence.
- Check with other parents about the situation.
- Don't fly off the handle with the teacher.
- Role play the interview with a friend before doing it. First play you, then the teacher.
- Find out if hitting children is permitted in the school in your area. Be clear about your right to protect your child from physical abuse. You may need to check out other schools and their discipline policies.

(See also **About Abuse**.)

Thanks to Evelyn Goodall, Circle from Calgary, Alberta, Canada

My child should be getting better grades. What shall I do?

- Spend time with her in reading and doing academic games. Stop when it is not fun.
- Ask her what she thinks about school and about learning. Listen carefully. Explain that *you* want her to do her best, and that does not mean she needs to be perfect.
- Tell her you will give her an agreed-upon reward if her grades start improving.
- Affirm her for Thinking and Doing. (See page 16.)
- Have her checked for learning disabilities. Many bright kids have specific learning differences.
- If this is a sudden change, make certain it is not a symptom of abuse or of drugs.
- Do not help with homework. That belongs to your child and the teacher.
- Make a rule that homework comes before play or television.
- The teacher's style of teaching may not match your child's learning needs. Find out if there is a teacher with another style of teaching.
- Spend ten to fifteen minutes a day with her using an attitude and study habits course such as *Straight Talk* by Robert Maidment. (See **Resources**.)

(See also D-1, D-3, D-8.)

Thanks to Harold Nordeman, Circle from Cincinnati, Ohio

My child worries constantly that he's not going to get his daily assignments done.

- Be sure he gets approval for the fun things he does when he is not doing homework.
- Schedule homework time with him and check at intervals to see what he has accomplished. Do *not* permit homework to be done at any other time.
- Find out what happens at school if a daily assignment is not done.
- Ask yourself if you have set up your life to work all the time and have little fun. If so, begin to enjoy life more yourself.
- Doing accomplishes more than worrying. Help him start doing so he'll have less time for worrying.
- Is he trying to be a perfect student? Will your family accept mistakes?
- Perhaps he has so many responsibilities at home that he doesn't get to his homework.
- Is he using his homework as a way to get out of doing chores?
- Give him lots of unconditional love.
- Ask his teacher if he is having a problem finishing things at school and so must do them at home.

(See also A-7, D-3, D-6, D-8.)

Thanks to Maggie Lawrence, Circle from Seattle, Washington

What can I say to my daughter when she puts herself down because she hasn't done well in her school work?

- Give her compliments about the things she does well.
- Say, "How come you are talking mean about someone I love?"
- Tell her, "You don't have to get A's for me to love you."
- Say, "Do your best in school, and that is fine."
- Say over and over, "I like you the way you are, and I like to see you grow."
- Show her ways in which you think, try new things, make mistakes, and change.
- Explain, "Everyone makes mistakes. Mistakes don't make you a bad person. They tell you what to improve."
- Say, "We don't hurt people, and you are a very important person."
- Give her lots of love and encourage her to think about what kind of student she wants to be.
- Say, "Tell me three things you like about yourself."
- Disagree with her.

(See also C-10, D-3, D-6, D-7, G-1.)

Thanks to Annette Bodmer, Circle from Burnsville, Minnesota

I know my child needs special help from the school counselor or a tutor, but my wife won't hear of it.

- Do what is best for the child.
- Set up a meeting with your wife, your child, and your child's counselor.
- Tell your child, "I love you. You will get the special help you deserve."
- Ask your wife to think about why she objects and to discuss it. Perhaps she attaches some sort of stigma to getting help. Talk about all the ways people must rely on other people just to live.
- Go to a minister or doctor for help on how to handle your differences with your wife.
- Show your spouse in many ways, "You are lovable and capable and not a failure because our child needs help."
- Ask a relative or friend who has used counseling to talk to your wife and reassure her it is OK for your kid to get special help.
- Have the child tested to make sure she needs the help. Ask your wife to read the reports.

Thanks to Mary Kay Truitt, Circle from St. Paul, Minnesota

E. Skill Building

Recital

How can I get my child to try new things?

• Try new things yourself.
• Take her to art and science museums.
• Rehearse new experiences with her. You could use puppets or dolls to role-play the new activity.
• Send her to camp now and Outward Bound later.
• Tell her a story about a child or yourself as a child who was scared and went on to succeed.
• Read old myths, fairy tales, and biographies to her.
• Affirm her past successful experiences with new things.
• Stop talking about it with her, and in three months, check to see if she is trying more new things.
• Do some new things together.
• Instead of sending her off for the day with a "Take care of yourself," you could say, "Take a chance today."
• Point out people taking risks.
• Affirm her strengths and capabilities.
• Acknowledge risk-taking behavior whenever she exhibits it.

(See also D-1.)

Thanks to Sandra Sittko, Circle from St. Louis, Missouri

I want to make sure my child learns to use a computer. What are some ways I can do that?

• Ask her if she is ready for summer computer camp.
• Hire a high-school computer whiz to tutor her.
• People can learn to use computers at any age. Don't hurry her.
• Look at the school program. She should learn to use a computer at school.
• Buy a computer, learn how to use it yourself, and encourage the whole family to learn.
• Games teach computer familiarity. Go on from there.
• *When* your child bugs you for a computer, rent one for a month.

Thanks to Jean Clarke, Circle from Plymouth, Minnesota

It is important to me that my kids write thank-you notes. How can I help make it less of a chore for my nine- and twelve-year-olds?

• Buy thank-you notes and let them just sign their names.
• Don't correct what they write.
• Let them telephone their thanks.
• Tell them they don't have to like the gift; they just have to say thanks.
• Encourage them to be creative and design their own cards.
• Buy fun stationery.
• Look for opportunities to send or give thank-you notes to them.
• Let them record thank-you tapes or send thank-you pictures.
• Do your thank-you notes or letters while they do theirs and have a family "thank-you note affair."
• Make a family rule that thank-you notes or calls go out within three days after the gift is received.

Thanks to Bobbi Mlekodaj, Circle from Coon Rapids, Minnesota

My son sometimes acts in ways that turn people off. What can I do to help him eliminate these behaviors?

• Catch him being effective and praise him for it.
• Model the desired behavior.
• Challenge the child after he has turned people off and listen to his responses.
• Don't protect him from the consequences of his behavior.
• Describe your feelings about what happened and suggest alternatives. "I felt mad while you were making fun of Lynn's ideas. Try telling what you think without mentioning anyone else."
• Discuss the logical consequences of his behavior, saying, "People may not want to be with you." And point out his responsibility for his choices: "Only you can decide how you act."
• Ask him how he would feel if someone had acted that way around him.
• Ask him what he could have done differently.
• Say, "You are smart. You can think of other ways to get what you want."
• Borrow a tape recorder (audio or video) from the library. Tape his behavior, let him listen, and ask him if he'd like to change anything.

(See also B-4, B-6, C-6, E-7.)

Thanks to Bobbi Mlekodaj, Circle from Plymouth, Minnesota

My twelve-year-old gossips maliciously. What can I say or do to discourage this behavior?

- Remind her that a gossipy mouth can get the whole person in trouble.
- Give her the Being affirmations. (See page 16.)
- Tell her the story about gossip. Gossip is a person who opens a bag of feathers on a hill. The feathers randomly blow every which way and reach people Gossip did not intend them to reach. And further, all the feathers can never be recovered.
- Ask her to think about how she feels when someone gossips about her.
- Pick a regularly scheduled library night out. Help her find other things to talk about.
- Whenever you hear her gossiping about someone, ask her to make two positive statements about that person.
- Tell her that you will be glad when she changes the way she talks.
- Ask her to find another way to talk with people.
- Give her lots of love. Let her know she is important to you as a person, not for everything she does.
- Wake her up at three in the morning and insist that she tell you *all* the gossip. Then refuse to listen to gossip at any other time of the day.

(See also C-2, E-4, E-8.)

Thanks to Becky Monson, Circle from Plymouth, Minnesota

When my son doesn't do something right, he has a tantrum and he throws his eyeglasses—even in gym class. They are getting broken very often. What can I do about him?

- Why does he get angry in his classes and in gym? *Investigate!*
- Have a "cost" for broken glasses: no movies because he can't see, and part of his allowance to help pay for the glasses, etc.
- Talk to him about anger being an OK feeling. Have him come and tell you when he has dealt with anger appropriately.
- Eight-year-olds can recycle two-year-old stuff. Tell him it's OK to feel angry, but not OK to throw glasses. Give him lots of nurturing. (See the affirmations for Thinking, page 16.)
- Make him earn the money to pay for them.
- Let him use the Fuss Box when he is angry (see page 120). Then get him to finish a project that is less than perfect and accept it that way.
- Find out where the pressure is coming from for him to be perfect, and get it turned off.
- Empathize with him and allow him to be frustrated. Piaget says that when children go from stage to stage, there is a period of frustration, and the child needs to cope with this. The parent should not solve the problem or take away the frustration. (See **Resources**.)

(See also B-3, B-6, I-15.)

Thanks to Roxy Chuchna, Circle from Albert Lea, Minnesota

My ten-year-old son was caught stealing seventeen dollars from a friend at school. He lied for two days. Now we know about it. How can we confront him?

- Directly.
- Confront him directly and honestly in a civil manner, not as an attack. Let him know that what he did was wrong, and he will have to make amends for this, but that you still love and care for him. Inspire *guilt* not *shame*. Read Kaufman's book on *Shame*. (See **Resources**.)
- Tell him you know. Discuss a way to pay the money back, including an apology and a fine for stealing and lying.
- You go to the child and tell what you know. Then say, "Since I am legally and emotionally responsible for you, you are going to take the money back to your friend, and I am going with you." Then do it.
- Confront him with evidence; let him think up his own penalty—perhaps working it off.
- Let him know how important you think it is to be able to trust your friends.
- Read *Teaching Your Children About Money* by Chris Snyder. (See **Resources**.)

(See also B-1, E-4.)

Thanks to Samara Kemp, Circle from Modesto, California

How can I help my children communicate clearly?

- Look at the communication between yourself and other adults. Be sure you are showing them how.
- Ask, "What are you telling me?" Then listen carefully.
- Compliment them when they do communicate clearly.
- Ask, "What are you trying to say to me?"
- Take time, show an openness and willingness to listen. They may need to practice talking, especially if school doesn't encourage self-expression.
- Role-play your situation with them.
- Ask, "Is there something you want me to do besides listen?"
- Use Active Listening. (Read *Parent Effectiveness Training* by Thomas Gordon; see **Resources**.)
- Don't trap your children with questions to which you know the answers.
- Encourage them to be responsible for telling how they feel. Don't you tell them. Ask, "How do you feel about that?" instead of "That makes you mad, doesn't it?"

(See also B-6, I-2.)

Thanks to Yvonne Gustafson, Circle from Moundsview, Minnesota

My child has no sense of humor. How can I help him?

- Take the child to funny places and experience being funny with him.
- Perhaps he has a sense of humor that is different from yours.
- Humor is a creative act that requires permission and nurturing from those around him. Enjoy him and protect him from criticism.
- Catch your child being funny and compliment him on it.
- Are you able to give humorous messages but not receive them?
- Be sure that your own sense of humor isn't biting.
- When his jokes flop, don't put him down.
- Get him a book on humor.
- Don't mix humor with criticism.
- Look under "novelties" in the yellow pages and buy props.
- Don't laugh at things that hurt.
- Expose the child to funny people and let him know that you like them.
- Show your child your own sense of humor.
- Make sure that there is not one child in the family who is labeled "the" humorous one.

Thanks to Sherri Goldsmith, Circle from Plymouth, Minnesota

F. Values and Priorities

My ten-year-old wants one of those large, expensive cuddly dolls. I can't stand them. What can I do?

- Remember, ten-year-olds learn from playing with dolls.
- Is this a hang-up, or do you have a good reason?
- Discuss the popularity of these dolls and explain about "media hype" and about pressure to get what other kids have.
- Get the doll and use this opportunity to share what you know about infant care.
- Discuss your feelings and say "no."
- Ask yourself if you dislike the dolls because they might not be good for your child or for some other reason?
- Get the doll if it's so important to her. Getting what is the fad makes your child part of the gang. That is important to a ten-year-old.
- A ten-year-old could earn money for a doll.
- If you do buy it, tell her that you did so because you love her and that you will ask her later if it was worth it. Remember, she may learn that it is not important to have what her friends have.

(See also C-8.)

Thanks to Evelyn Goodall, Circle from Calgary, Alberta, Canada

I don't like the lyrics of the music my twelve-year-old boy listens to. What can I do?

• Tell him, "I'm feeling uncomfortable about the lyrics of the music you listen to. Let's sit down and talk about them."

• Tell him, "I'm not pleased with the words of the music to which you listen. I would like you to listen to music that has positive lyrics."

• Take him to holiday concerts. Go to church and sing together. Encourage him to sing in choir or learn to play a musical instrument.

• Say, "No, I don't want you to listen to that."

• Ask, "Have you thought about the meaning of the words? Can we discuss them?"

• Offer other types of music for him to listen to and then invite him to listen with you.

• Ask him to write down the lyrics and read them to you or to another adult. Then ask if that is what he wants to put into his head.

• Ask him how he thinks people would be living ten years from now if they do what the lyrics say.

(See also B-4.)

Thanks to Evelyn Goodall, Circle from Calgary, Alberta, Canada

My uncle is not expected to live long. We have not talked about death. What do I say and how can I prepare my children for the funeral?

• Explain it as fully as you can. Tell them older people usually die before younger ones, grandparents before parents.

• Tell them that every living thing in the world dies sometime and many older people are ready to die when they die.

• Tell them that some people live long lives and some people live short lives. Uncle has lived a long life.

• You can get some help with your own grieving by reading *Life Is Goodbye Life Is Hello* by Alla Bozarth-Campbell. (See **Resources**.)

• Take the children to visit your uncle while he is alive.

• Tell them about or have them participate in all the activities of the funeral.

• Encourage them to play funeral with their dolls.

• Express your own sadness. Ask them to comfort you when they feel like it.

• Arrange to have each child have something to remember him by.

• Read *My Grandpa Died Today* by Joan Fassler or *The Dead Bird* by Margaret Brown. (See **Resources**.)

(See also F-4.)

Thanks to Jean Clarke, Circle from Plymouth, Minnesota

My fifteen-year-old nephew committed suicide. Shall we tell the children how he died, or shall we protect them until they are older?

- Be honest with the kids, or they will find out and will wonder why you lied.
- Talk with the kids about what death means to them and how they feel about it.
- Have a discussion with your kids about suicide. This could be an insurance policy against it.
- Use this as an opportunity to discuss feelings about death with your children.
- Help your children look at how suicide affects family and friends.
- Tell them. Encourage them not to blame your nephew as they do not know what was going on in his mind.
- Discuss with the kids the whys of suicide and the alternatives.
- Many adolescents commit suicide. Make sure your children know that suicide does not solve problems.
- Ask your minister, rabbi, or priest to talk about suicide in the service, and then talk to your children.
- Remember that family secrets are usually destructive.

(See also F-3.)

Thanks to Kay Kubes, Circle from St. Paul, Minnesota

My children seem fearful of nuclear war. When they see something about it on TV, they clam up or do something disruptive. What should I do?

- Encourage them to talk about it and ask how they feel about it.
- Watch the show with them and ask how they feel about it. If they cry, let them cry.
- Turn off the TV and say, "I want to talk about what we just saw. Will you talk with me?"
- Ask what they have learned about it in school.
- Give them puppets and ask them to have the puppets tell you how they feel about nuclear war.
- Call your children's school and ask if they will do something to help all the students with these fears.
- Be sure you feel comfortable talking about it. If you don't, find some friends or go to a conference where you can practice talking and listening about it.
- Tell them how you feel.

Thanks to Jean Clarke, Circle from Wayzata, Minnesota

My sister drinks a lot. My son mentioned it to her, and I'm embarrassed. What can I do?

- I hope you are not embarrassed for your son. You may be embarrassed for your sister or yourself. You can discuss with your child that alcoholism is an illness and that the family can help her.
- Your son did what you should have done before this. Tell him it is OK to notice what is really happening.
- Pat him on the back and tell him it's important to be honest about feelings and thank him for helping get this difficult issue into the open.
- This would be a perfect time to have a discussion with your sister.
- Contact Al-Anon and seek out support for you and your child.
- If you're embarrassed, you may have been brought up to believe the "secrecy rule" about not seeing alcoholism. You need to examine your own rules.
- Talk with the other family members who have been affected by her drinking. As a group, confront her and offer a plan for what she can do to overcome her problem.

(See also H-8, H-9.)

Thanks to Sandra Sittko, Circle from St. Paul, Minnesota

Our family has gone to church only sporadically. Now, as parents, we have decided that it is important for the whole family to go to church. The eleven-year-old hassles and the eight-year-old is scared. What can we do?

- Tell the children, "We have decided that you will go to church because it is important for all of us. You have the choice of sitting quietly in church or going to Sunday school."
- Tell the children, "We have decided that you will go to church for one year because it is an important part of our lives. After church each week we will discuss your feelings and what you learned."
- Invite the minister and Sunday school teacher for a social activity or dinner.
- Find out if the kids have any friends who already go to the church you plan to attend. If not, tell them that they can take a friend to Sunday school.
- After church, look for other family activities. Go out for brunch, ice cream, or to the zoo. Make Sunday a family fun day.
- Tell them calmly that you are all going to church once a week but some weeks they can choose which church activity to attend.
- Visit churches for a month together. At the end of the month, choose a church together.

Thanks to Jeanette Hickman-Kingsley, Circle from Minnetonka, Minnesota

G. Building Self-Esteem

What can I do to encourage my children to be responsible for their own self-esteem?

• Hang a bulletin board in each of their rooms for them to post whatever is important to them. Mention what you see.

• Ask for positive messages for yourself. They will pick it up from hearing you do it. If you keep your self-esteem high, they'll see how to do it.

• Teach them to separate helpful negative comments from destructive criticism and to keep only what's helpful.

• Encourage them to talk about their large and small triumphs.

• Be able to accept compliments yourself.

• Together, write down positive things about themselves and post the sheets.

• Have their bedtime ritual include, "Four things I did well today are. . . ."

• Teach them to ask for hugs when they want them.

• Play the "Ups and Downs with Feelings" game with them. (See the last page of this book for more information.)

• Don't force them to compete with the rest of the family. Let them be unique.

• Read them Affirmations for Growth and encourage them to ask for the ones they want each day. (See page 14.)

(See also C-10, G-7.)

Thanks to Kathy Brinkerhoff, Circle from Lafayette, California

My child sets himself up to be criticized. How can I help him?

- Ask yourself if this is the only way he gets attention from you and others.
- Watch the way he sets you up to criticize him. Point out his part in asking for criticism, and refuse to give the negative messages.
- Check to see if you are overly critical toward your son or yourself.
- Visualize him believing all the good stuff about himself, and visualize yourself as a nurturing and caring parent.
- Go ahead and give him lots of reinforcement that tells him you like him just the way he is.
- Tell him five things you like about him before he goes to bed each night.
- Be careful you don't give helpful messages in a critical voice.
- Read *Self-Esteem: A Family Affair.* Learn about the four ways of parenting; then stick to giving him the positive Nurturing and Structuring messages. (See **Resources**.)
- Catch him being good. Compliment him when you see him doing it the way you want him to.

(See also D-4, E-4, G-1.)

Thanks to Toni Drucker, Circle from Orinda, California

**How do I as a parent help my child learn to reject
negative messages and teasing at school?**

- Don't accept negative messages yourself and
  don't give them yourself.
- Read *Self-Esteem: A Family Affair* to learn
  about the four ways of parenting, and give lots of
  positive messages at home. (See **Resources**.)
- Teach the child specifically to ignore or to refuse
  to accept negative messages. Have him practice
  saying, "I don't accept that," when he hears a
  negative message.
- Ask the teacher to work with the whole class on
  rejecting verbal abuse and teasing and how to
  cope with both.
- Suggest to the principal that the whole school
  plan a self-esteem week.
- Affirm him. Say, "You are a worthwhile person.
  I love and respect you."
- Tell him that he doesn't have to believe the
  negative messages, and that he can look for a
  kernel of truth in what people are telling him.
- Have him make a list of things he likes about
  himself. Invite everyone in the family to add to
  the list. Post it where he can see it every day.
- Teach him to throw hurtful stuff in the garbage
  can. You can do the same.

(See also D-2, D-4, G-2.)

Thanks to Deane Gradous, Circle from Wayzata,
Minnesota

My eleven-year-old thinks that he knows everything. He won't take advice or instruction from anyone. What can I do?

- Provide him with some tougher challenges.
- Ask him to take charge of some family situations and support his leadership role without giving advice. He will find out that there are some things he doesn't know.
- I have yet to meet an eleven-year-old who knows everything. Are you buying into this fiction in some way?
- Let him fail and take the full consequences of failure without your interfering.
- As a responsible parent, you decide when to insist that things be done a certain way.
- When he is being successful, let him continue. Tell him to ask for help if he needs it.
- Give him affirmations for six- to twelve-year-olds like "You can find a way of doing things that works for you." (See page 14.)
- Try saying, "I feel...." or "For me it works to...." instead of being authoritarian and saying, "Do it this way," or "You should do it this way."
- Let him do things away from home—Scouts, science center. Have him make his own arrangements. Give him opportunities to discover that things are not always as simple as they seem.

Thanks to Linda Buranen, Circle from Plymouth, Minnesota

Our ten-year-old daughter puts herself down because she sees herself as overweight. Television feeds this image. How can we support her to accept herself as she is?

- Acknowledge that she thinks she is overweight. Assure her that you love her. Together, check with the doctor on an appropriate weight for her.
- Every day, give her positive messages *not* related to eating, food, body size, or appearance.
- Collect facts related to dieting. Be aware of problems related to food abuse, such as anorexia nervosa and bulimia.
- Health is a primary concern. How do you handle your own self-image and control your own weight?
- Give her the affirmations for Being. (See page 16.)
- Make sure that her eating is healthy and in control. Then shift the focus of your concern away from food issues.
- Check to see if she feels in control of other areas of her life (not only her weight).
- Suggest exercise to increase tone and energy. Take a fitness class together.

(See also H-1.)

Thanks to Gail Davenport, Circle from Edmonds, Washington

My child hits or scolds himself when he is frustrated or unable to handle a situation. What can I do to help him take better care of himself?

- People grow from their strengths. Emphasize his.
- Whenever you see him hurting himself, say, "Stop that!" and then tell him you expect him to take care of himself.
- Say, "Don't hit yourself. I care about you."
- Ask, "What could you do instead of ragging on yourself?"
- Look for lots of ways to let him know you love him.
- Ask him, "Why do you think you should be able to handle *every* situation? Nobody else can."
- Give him an empty milk carton or pillow to kick or hit instead.
- Let him see you handling your own frustrations without scolding yourself or others.
- Remind him of the house rule "We don't hurt people."
- Say, "If you feel like hitting yourself, try this Fuss Box instead." (See page 120.)

(See also E-6, E-9.)

Thanks to Sue Hansen, Circle from Bellevue, Washington

My children don't believe they are responsible for how their days go. What can I say instead of "Have a good day"?

- How about "I love you! Build yourself a good day."
- "I hope you accomplish a lot today."
- "Today is another challenge."
- "My love goes with you today. Make it a good one."
- "I wish you a wonderful day."
- Give them a kiss and a hug and tell them, "I hope you learn lots today."
- "Make today really special."
- "I'll be looking forward to hearing about your day when you get home."
- Saying, "Make yourself a good day," encourages them to take the responsibility for their day.
- "Learn something new today."
- "Smell the flowers."
- "Shalom."
- "Find something interesting today."
- Tuck a loving message in their pockets or lunch boxes.
- Invite them to "enjoy school."

(See also G-1.)

Thanks to Sandra Sittko, Circle from St. Louis, Missouri

H. Health and Wellness, Differences and Drugs

My eight-year-old daughter is overweight. What can I do or say to help her?

- Have a variety of fruit and vegetables around the house to satisfy her appetite after school.
- Buy stickers instead of food for treats.
- Catch her succeeding at eating correctly and compliment her for that.
- Ask your daughter what help she wants from you.
- Take her to the grocery store so she can pick new foods that are low in fat and healthy.
- Ask her to check with herself whether she is eating for fun or boredom or hunger and then to eat only when hungry.
- Find nutritional, low-calorie recipes and try them together with her.
- How about modeling? Are other family members overweight? Do they exercise?
- Catch her succeeding when she is substituting fun activities instead of eating.
- Give her lots of Being messages and find time to be with her. (See page 16.)
- Make exercise a habit and a fun and enjoyable part of the daily routine.
- You have control of what you provide for eating in your house. Offer healthy, low-calorie food and snacks.

(See also B-7, G-5.)

Thanks to Nat Houtz, Circle from Lynwood, Washington

My son is eight years old and still wets the bed most nights. He can't go to sleepovers, and I'm tired of doing all the wash and smelling urine all the time. What can I do?

- Talk to your physician.
- Realize that bedwetting is a problem of sleeping too deeply, and as his nervous system matures, he'll wake up to go.
- Have your son change his own sheets and put the sheets in the washing machine and start it.
- Create a program of going to the bathroom at bedtime.
- Reassure him. Tell him that he is not the only boy this age to have this problem.
- See if your child wants an alarm to get up with to go to the bathroom during the night. He has to manage it.
- Assure the child that you love him no matter what.
- Do not ever ridicule the child. You can tell him that *you* have a problem with the extra laundry.
- If your doctor says there is no organic reason, check for stress in your son's life. Child and family counselors are available to help.
- Remember Michael Landon did this, too.

Thanks to Kay Kubes, Circle from St. Paul, Minnesota

My sixth-grade boy is short and a slow developer. The boys in physical education class keep bugging him. How can I help?

- Suggest that he talk to his P.E. teacher. Ask him if he wants you to be there too.
- Ask for a conference with the school counselor.
- Remind the child to give himself time. He has a growth spurt coming up.
- Talk about neat men who happen to be short.
- Ask the doctor for a normal growth chart and show him how wide the normal range is.
- Tell him about any men you now know who developed late and are happy now.
- Have him take gymnastics, free-style skiing, or soccer. Small boys have an advantage in those sports.
- Have him take karate or judo to learn to protect himself and to build self-confidence.
- Treat him according to his age, not his size.

Thanks to Gail Nordeman, Circle from Cincinnati, Ohio

My fifth-grade daughter has developed early. She wears a bra for comfort. The girls tease her, and the boys snap her bra straps. How can I help her?

• Tell her firmly and confidently that she is normal, that she is an early developer. She's OK. Others will catch up. Read Peter Mayle's *What's Happening to Me?* with her. (See **Resources**.)

• Show her that each child will be different in some ways, that is, tall or short, and still be normal.

• Talk about how it was for you when you were a child so she does not feel alone.

• Say, "I love you the way you are, and your body is developing just the right way for you."

• Treat her like a fifth grader, not older. Don't rush her growing up to match her body.

• If your family physician is empathetic, ask for support from him or her.

• Teach her to evaluate teasing for what it says about the other person.

• Tell her she is in charge of setting boundaries for her own body and that she can tell people when to *keep their hands off.*

• Go to school and tell the staff that the boys' behavior is not acceptable.

• Be sure both mother and father affirm daughter's changes.

(See also G-3.)

Thanks to Jean Clarke, Circle from Plymouth, Minnesota

My child has asthma and looks like the other kids, but this condition creates many problems, like missing school, low energy, etc. How can I help?

- Tell your child she is wonderful, capable, and lovable. Give her lots of hugs!
- Look for stories or articles about people who have asthma and accomplish great things.
- Make certain her medical care is the best available for the problem.
- Learn all you can about asthma and its management and teach this to her.
- Go to school and ask the school nurse to talk to the class about how kids need to manage their various medical problems, not just asthma.
- Make quiet activities meaningful and constructive.
- Tell her that it's OK to let other people know how she feels and what she needs.
- Teach her not to accept thoughtless, critical messages about her health.
- Acknowledge that she is different in some ways and the same in most ways.
- Regularly and often discuss the many ways she enjoys life.
- Expect her to manage her health and support and help her while she learns how.
- Send her to a camp for asthmatic children.

(See also G-3.)

Thanks to Mary Kay Truitt, Circle from St. Paul, Minnesota

How can I handle my son's reactions and sensitive feelings after being criticized by a boy in the neighborhood? My son has a repaired cleft lip.

- Tell him, "You look wonderful to *me*!"
- Train him to ignore such remarks and go on playing.
- Tell him to ignore this criticism and to stay away from that boy.
- Talk to the other boy's parents about the situation.
- Say, "I'm sorry he did that. He must not know much about cleft lips."
- Say, "Well, he could have been born with a cleft lip himself. Maybe he hasn't thought about that."
- Say, "I love all of you, and your lip is part of you."
- Say, "Wow! He hasn't learned very good manners yet, has he?"
- Suggest he say, "No big deal. Let's play."

(See also G-3.)

Thanks to Gail Davenport, Circle from Lynwood, Washington

The liquor in my cupboard is disappearing faster than I think it should. My twelve-year-old son's friends are in the house a lot; I'm afraid they're drinking it.

- Confront your son directly. Ask him about the situation. Decide with him how to handle it.
- Supervise play when his friends are in the house.
- Tell your son, "The liquor is going down faster than I'm using it. Adults use liquor and children don't. You and your friends are *not* to take any of it."
- If his friends are drinking it, share your suspicions with their parents and get their support in stopping the drinking.
- Tell him you know about the problem and put Ipecac in one of the bottles. (Ipecac is a non-prescription drug that makes you vomit.)
- Lock the liquor cabinet.
- Teach him about the disease of alcoholism. Learn about it yourself, if you don't know.
- Tell him that alcohol is much more damaging to a growing liver than it is to a mature one. The damage could be life-threatening and permanent.

(See also F-6, H-8, H-9.)

Thanks to Jean Clarke, Circle from Minneapolis, Minnesota

My eleven-year-old son wants to have a glass of wine with us at holiday dinners. Should we give it to him?

• Make a decision that is comfortable for you. Make sure he is clear about your decision.
• Alcohol is not appropriate for an eleven-year-old.
• Wait until the legal drinking age according to your state.
• Say, "No." Stick to it.
• Be clear about which traditional holidays and which children may have a glass of wine. Stick to it.
• With alcoholism a major problem in this country, why should anyone start drinking at eleven?
• If there is no alcoholism in your family, follow your family tradition. If there is, why have it at all?
• Provide an alternative, such as grape juice or catawba juice.
• Is wine necessary for anyone at this meal?

(See also F-6, H-7, H-9.)

Thanks to Sandra Sittko, Circle from St. Paul, Minnesota

My friend called and said she had found marijuana in her boy's pocket. Her boy is my son's best friend.

- Thank her for telling you. Confront your son.
- Say to your son, "Your friend is in trouble. How can we help him? This is serious!"
- Don't get defensive. Ask your son if he and his friend have used marijuana and if he is ready to talk about it.
- After explaining to your son what you know, explain the legal risks of using marijuana and the consequences in your family.
- Take care not to take this casually or to act as if it is humorous.
- Explain the health hazards and consequences of marijuana use.
- Look to your own use of drugs, medications, and alcohol. Is there a need for change?
- Call the school and ask if they know of drug use or sources at school.
- Form a support group with other parents and discuss this.
- Encourage the school to incorporate a drug abuse prevention program.
- Tell your son how important he is to you and how concerned you are.
- Contact the National Clearinghouse for Drug Abuse Information. (See **Resources**.)

(See also F-6, H-7, H-8.)

Thanks to Christine Ternand, Circle from Minneapolis, Minnesota

I. The Job of the Parent

It seems to me that my older children are taking over my role as parent with the younger children. What shall I do?

- Describe what they are doing and then intervene and tell them you are in charge.
- To some extent this is normal. They are learning and practicing being responsible. However, be sure to set limits. For example, discipline and final decisions are up to the parents.
- Discuss with the children your responsibilities and theirs. Thank them for their assistance in taking care of themselves and one another.
- Ask yourself: Have I given up my parenting role? Am I afraid to have them grow up and gain responsibility? Is what they are doing really OK?
- Say, "I am the parent."
- Ask them to switch roles with you for twenty minutes and take care of you instead of bossing the little kids.
- Give them lots of nurturing and reward the positive parenting skills you see them developing.
- Tell them you love them and appreciate their good parenting skills. Remind them that you are responsible for being the parent.

Thanks to Deane Gradous, Circle from Wayzata, Minnesota

What are some ways an adult can be respectful to children, to set an example for them?

- Give them privacy.
- Don't talk down to them. Talk at eye level.
- Show courtesy, respect, and empathy for them, and expect them to give you the same.
- Share rule-setting.
- Listen to what they have to say. Ask about events and problems that are important to them. Ask their opinions.
- Keep your promises and follow through on rules.
- Compliment them on things they do well and tell them how much you love them.
- Respect others and yourself. Be honest. Be kind and understanding. Explain your actions and feelings.
- Introduce them by name to friends and acquaintances.
- Admit your mistakes and apologize when you are wrong.
- Say, "Please and thank you."
- Everytime I switch roles with my son for a few minutes, we both learn oodles about being more respectful to each other.
- Tell the kids what to expect.
- Only have secrets that are fun for all of you.

Thanks to Suzanne Morgan, Circle from Albert Lea, Minnesota

How can I avoid power struggles with my ten-year-old son? He hassles me and yells a lot.

- Bring his behavior to his attention and tell him how you feel about it.
- Assess what he is trying to tell you with his behavior. Is he in competition with you? For what?
- Change *your* behavior for one week. Refuse to push or nag. Observe the results.
- Reward any signs of cooperation.
- Check with other parents to see if his behavior is in the range of normal.
- Limit yourself to giving him three suggestions a day. Ask him to try out one suggestion. Reward him when he changes his behavior.
- Double the number of hugs that you give him.
- Spend time playing with him.
- Refuse to negotiate non-negotiable rules.
- Hassle with him in a loving way when you feel good. If you don't know how to hassle, you can find out in *Self-Esteem: A Family Affair* by Jean Illsley Clarke. (See **Resources**.)
- Kids this age need to hassle about rules. You might think about how much hassling you are willing to do on any given day.
- Ask him to yell other places like in the closet or shower.

(See also C-6.)

Thanks to Sandra Sittko, Circle from St. Louis, Missouri

How can I as a parent stay peaceful in the midst of my child's complaining, hassling, and put downs?

- Have the child write or draw her complaints for you to see.
- When she starts, wear ear plugs, when she stops take them out and tell her to ask for what she wants directly.
- Sing.
- Let her know that her behavior bothers you and you are working on its not bothering you.
- Think about what you want to express instead of irritation and do it. Try affirmations instead of yelling.
- Practice centering with her. Refer to *The Centering Book* by Hendricks and Wills. (See **Resources**.)
- Make a "no put-down" rule for the entire family and enforce it.
- Visualize your family cooperating in a loving, fun way.
- Take better care of yourself; spend time alone; get the rest and exercise you need.
- Avoid complaining and hassling yourself for a while.

(See also I-2.)

Thanks to Ellen Peterson, Circle from Lafayette, California

My child doesn't often tell me about things that happen to him. How can I get him to tell me? I think parents should know what is going on.

- Model trust by sharing things with your spouse in front of the child.
- Set aside five to ten minutes a day with the child and invite him to talk about anything he wants to talk about. Affirm him for talking to you.
- Be trustworthy. Don't betray his confidences.
- When he does talk, be sure not to interrupt or ridicule.
- Let's face it. Our children will never tell us everything. However, if you have a trusting relationship, the important things will come out.
- Talk to your kids about your life.
- Rhea Zakich's *The Ungame* really gets everyone talking and sharing. It is not competitive in any way and is very non-threatening. (See **Resources**.)
- Ask him about what has been happening in his life. If he chooses not to share anything with you, show him you love him and tell him you will ask again because you care about him.
- Use Active Listening Techniques. Read Thomas Gordon's *Parent Effectiveness Training*. (See **Resources**.)

(See also I-2.)

Thanks to Sandra Sittko, Circle from St. Paul, Minnesota

I discussed my child's problem with my doctor and I just don't feel comfortable with what she says we should do. What do I do now?

- Consult another physician.
- Discuss your concerns with family and friends and ask what they would do.
- If the doctor is a good listener, state your concerns to her.
- If this is not life threatening, try what you have been told by your physician. It may work.
- Trust your intuition.
- Check to see if you heard right.
- Ask a nurse with whom you feel comfortable what she thinks of your concern.
- If the problem is urgent, do something. Don't stay in indecision.
- Realize that doctors are people, too. They don't have all the answers.
- Look up information on the problem at the library and see if her treatment plan corresponds with recent material on the subject.
- Ask your doctor if there are other medical viewpoints on the problem.
- Trust your feelings about the doctor. If you trust her, try what she suggests; if not, find someone you do trust.

Thanks to Kay Kubes, Circle from St. Paul, Minnesota

My in-laws interfere by hinting that my kids shouldn't have to follow family rules. How can I deal with them when we are face to face?

- Be your own person. Say, "At our house, parents make the rules and the children must follow them."
- Let them know that your family has decided on rules for living as a family.
- Say, "We expect our children to follow our family rules. Do not encourage the children to break rules."
- Ask, "Will you help me by reinforcing the family rules when I am not here?" (If they decline, find ways to shorten the visits.)
- Post a few of the family rules on the refrigerator. Point them out to your in-laws.
- Ask your spouse to tell them to turn it off.
- Notice things they do well with the children and compliment them.
- Rethink your rules. Maybe you will decide that your in-laws are right about some of them.
- When they drop hints, clap your hands over your ears and say, "I hope the children didn't hear that."

(See also B-8.)

Thanks to Carole Gesme, Circle from Minnetonka, Minnesota

My in-laws criticize me and the children. I want to stop this, but I don't want to alienate them. Do you have any suggestions?

- Tell them you love and appreciate their interest but that their messages may be damaging to your children.
- When they criticize, tell them in a matter-of-fact tone, "Criticism hurts. I want you to tell her when she does well."
- Next time you are with them, give two positive messages to each person there, including yourself and your child. Stay busy doing that.
- Trust your feelings to know what to do. You may need to tell your family how you feel.
- Teach your child how to reject unhelpful or negative messages. Compliment her about how well she does that.
- Read *Ouch, That Hurts!* by Jean Illsley Clarke and use the parts that will help you and your child. (See **Resources**.)
- Ask them to be kind instead of critical.
- Tell them you are learning how to be directive without being critical and you want them to practice with you.
- When they send a zapper to you say, "Ouch" or fall down on the floor and say, "I'm wounded."
- Have your children wear buttons or T-shirts that say, "Be gentle. Human being inside."

(See also C-2.)

Thanks to Pearl Noreen, Circle from Seattle, Washington

My spouse and I are getting a divorce. I'm upset about it. How can I help the kids?

- Get help for yourself first. Go to a support group or counselor.
- Tell your kids that you and your spouse are getting a divorce because you two can no longer live together and that it is NOT their fault.
- Tell the truth. Don't make it worse or better than it really is.
- Ask them what they need and get that for them if you can. Answer the children's questions directly.
- Think how to get support for the kids. Now's the time to turn to grandparents, aunts, uncles, and friends.
- Spend extra time with the kids when you are feeling good.
- Find out if there is a support group at school for kids whose parents are going through a divorce.
- See *The Kids' Book of Divorce* by Eric Rofes. If you are fighting, get *Something Is Wrong at My House* by Diane Davis. (See **Resources**.)
- Tell them, "Because we can't live together doesn't mean we will love you any less."
- Order the free booklet, *Helping Children Face Crises* by Alicerose Barman. (See **Resources**.)

Thanks to Sandra Sittko, Circle from St. Louis, Missouri

My stepson resents my being in charge of him. He ignores me and is negative toward me. What can I do?

- Offer him unconditional love without expecting him to return the same to you.
- Say to him, "What you need is important to me" and "I'm glad I know you." (See page 16.)
- Affirm yourself as a worthwhile person. Don't take his attacks personally. Require him to abide by the established family rules.
- Consistent, skillful parenting pays off in establishing a bond with a child who did not ask you to be his stepmother. Keep at it, not at him.
- Expect your spouse to help insist that your stepson follow rules while he is with you.
- Let him know you are not afraid of his anger.
- Remember that building your relationship with him will take time. Get support from others during this period.
- Consider how he is feeling about the situation. Encourage him to talk about how he is feeling.
- Be careful that each of you has private space and time in your work.
- Visualize the family as you want it to be in two years.

Thanks to Nat Houtz, Circle from Lynwood, Washington

**I have to go to work. How can I find good before-
and after-school care for my child?**

- Chat with mothers in the neighborhood or apartment building; find out who they use and what they look for in a caregiver.
- Look for a neighbor with children about the same age who might care for your child.
- Check with the schools for latchkey programs.
- Call churches to see if they have lists of qualified sitters.
- Call your county welfare agency for the names of licensed day-care providers. Interview several providers before deciding.
- Ask a neighbor who is at home with an infant if he or she would welcome an older child twice a day.
- Put an ad in the church bulletin or other local publication.
- Get references. Trust your feelings about the setting that will be best for your child.

Thanks to Roxanne Michelson, Circle from St. Paul, Minnesota

I'm beginning to resent that I am doing too much for the rest of the family, but they expect me to. How can I change that?

- Compliment them when someone in the family does something for you.
- Establish a specific amount of time for yourself every day.
- Have a family meeting; present your problem and ask for suggestions.
- Look at your expectations to see if they are reasonable. Don't get white carpets if you have four kids under twelve.
- Teach others how to do chores. Teach one chore at a time.
- If it is someone else's job, leave it undone.
- Put a notice on the refrigerator:
  Dear Children,
  I have changed. Please notice that I no longer
  _____. Please compliment me when I
  _____.
- Remember, kids don't have to like doing chores, they just have to do them.
- Assign chores to each child. Make a coupon book of chore coupons for each and allow one day a week when each child gives you the coupon and you do the chore for him or her as a special favor. This will teach children that your help is a gift, not a right.

Thanks to Betty Beach, Circle from Minnetonka Beach, Minnesota

115

How do I get my kids to respect my right to have some time alone with my friends or on the phone?

- Say, "We'll have time together when I'm done." Follow through on your promise and spend time with them when you are off the phone or when the guests are gone.
- Be firm and fair. If they disrupt a phone call, tell them, "This is my time. Your time was earlier or will come later. Don't interrupt me again. I respect your time and I expect you to respect my time."
- Negotiate rules and guidelines to be followed by everyone in the family. Tell them that you need time separate from them and that they are also entitled to privacy.
- Keep a timer by the phone so that you keep your phone calls the length you want.
- Set aside one hour a day when you are to be left alone. I know a mom with eight kids who does it, so I know it can work.
- Tell them what you think and what they are to do while you are on the phone such as "When I have friends over, you are to give me thirty minutes of uninterrupted time. Let me know if you are hurt or in trouble, otherwise play by yourselves."
- Respect their rights and expect them to respect yours. Set consequences for when they don't.

Thanks to Ellen Peterson, Circle from Walnut Creek, California

**My neighbors were talking about molesting and
incest. I wonder if this could be the root of my
daughter's behavior problems. I'm scared about
this.**

- You can think about this and not let your fear
  stop your thinking. You can talk to a counselor
  or doctor.
- Tell your daughter you expect her to trust her
  feelings and to tell you if anything doesn't feel
  right.
- Talk to her gently and nurturingly.
- Ask your daughter to draw a picture of your
  family, then you look for what the picture says
  about her place in the family.
- Teach her that harmful secrets are not OK.
  Only problems that are known can be solved.
- Talk to your doctor.
- Talk to a counselor or someone at Child
  Protective Services about your fears.
- Believe that your daughter is telling you
  something with her behavior. Stick with it until
  you find out what it is. If not incest, it is
  something else.
- Read *No More Secrets for Me* by Oralee
  Wachter with your daughter. Read *No More
  Secrets* by Caren Adams and Jennifer Fay for
  lots of specific things you can do. Newman's
  Never Say Yes to a Stranger is helpful. (See
  Resources.)

Thanks to Mary Kay Truitt, Circle from St. Paul,
Minnesota

How can I handle my anger with my child?

• Talk to someone you trust.
• Keep an anger journal. Write down your feelings.
• Don't yell. Focus on solving the problem. Come back to the subject.
• Listen and ask the child, "What do you need?"
• Take a walk.
• Think! Figure out what will help resolve the problem. Then do it.
• Remember three great things about your child to help you put your anger in perspective.
• Give responsibility for the problem to the child if he is behaving badly.
• Delete expletives.
• Affirm yourself. Say, "I am a lovable and loving person," ten times.
• Remember, your worth as a person is separate from what your child does.
• Get a cup of coffee and collect your thoughts and emotions.
• Own your feelings. Use "I" statements.
• Use the Fuss Box. (See page 120.)
• Stop and think.
• Learn about child development to see if you are expecting too much. (See pages 6 and 9.)

(See also B-1.)

Thanks to Harold Nordeman, Circle from Cincinnati, Ohio

While my seven-year-old daughter was being cared for by a seventeen-year-old neighbor girl, the neighbor girl went with her mother to get her hair cut and left my daughter with the father and sixteen-year-old brother. The brother and my daughter went up to the boy's bedroom. While they were there, my daughter said, the boy told her to put her hand on him. She did and said, "That's your penis!" He said, "No, it's not; it's a picture frame." She said, "That's your penis" and went downstairs. I told my daughter she'd done well. What shall I do about the babysitter?

- Tell the girl and her parents that the daughter can babysit only at your home because either their son approached your daughter or your daughter fantasized the episode. They can decide what to do.
- Have the girl sit only at your house with a "No Visitors" rule.
- Call your local child protection service.
- Address the boy directly. If he denies it and will not accept responsibility, then his parents should be responsible to get help for him.
- Write down all the messages you have in your mind about a situation like this. Pick out the ones that are helpful and act on them.
- Confront him.
- Remember, if you don't confront the boy, other children may be unnecessarily victimized.
- Tell him in front of his parents.

Thanks to Bobbi Mlekodaj, Circle from Minneapolis, Minnesota

The Fuss Box

A Fuss Box is a place to vent your anger so you can think clearly about what to do to help yourself or others.

The purpose of the Fuss Box is to help people
- claim their anger,
- claim their right to express anger,
- claim responsibility for anger,
- have a way to express anger without hurting themselves or other people and without other people interfering with the expression of anger or trying to "fix" it, and
- have a way to clear out the anger and get on with solutions to the problems.

How do you make a Fuss Box? Find a sturdy box or carton big enough to stand in with a bit of space to move around. Write FUSS BOX in bold letters on all sides of the box so that anyone entering the room while you are fussing will be reminded that you are to be left alone because you are in the Fuss Box.

How do you use the Fuss Box? First, let everyone in your family group (or wherever you use the box) know the purpose of the box and the rules for using it. Write the rules on a poster that you bring out whenever you use the box.

Fuss Box Rules
1. Choose the place with care.
2. Stay in the box while fussing.
3. Say whatever you want to.
4. Other people do not interfere.
5. Fuss until you feel your energy switch.
6. Then step out of the box and decide how to make the situation better.

These Rules Are Important

1. Select with care the place where you will use the box. Use it only in a place where people care about you. Do not use it in front of young children who may not understand what you are doing or might be frightened. Don't use it in front of people who might use what you said to "get you" later.
2. Stand in the box while you are fussing.
3. Say anything you want to. Your words may be unreasonable, unwarranted, or unfair. Express your frustrations.
4. Other people are to stay out of it. They can sympathize, but they are not to argue or try to fix or console you. They have to leave the room if they are tempted to feel any hurt, fear, or responsibility for your feelings.
5. Fuss as vigorously as you want until you feel your energy switch, usually from about thirty seconds to four or five minutes. When you start to feel calm or chuckle at yourself, say, "I feel better now" and step outside the box.

6. Stand beside the Fuss Box and decide at least one thing you will do to make the situation better. Do it.

CAUTION: Do not step outside the box and continue to fuss. If you do that, get back into the box and do your fussing there. Otherwise, you can encourage yourself to continue fussing instead of solving problems.

CAUTION: Use a real box. People who do not use a real box are not setting clear boundaries.

CAUTION: Do not use the Fuss Box just to vent anger and/or frustration and then do nothing about the situation. That would be using the box to encourage your frustration and to make life worse instead of better. Use the Fuss Box for ordinary frustrations. Get help from a counselor if you have deep rage.

The Fuss Box can be used with six- to twelve-year-old children. Insist that they and you follow the rules whenever the Fuss Box is used.

—Jean Illsley Clarke

Where to Go for Additional Support

If you have talked with your family and friends, tried the ideas in the Suggestion Circle, read some child-rearing books, and still feel stuck with a problem, here are some places to call for additional help or to find out about parenting classes. If you have difficulty finding a phone number after looking in both the white and the yellow pages, call any of these sources and ask them to help you find the phone number you need.

Community Services

Crisis or hot-line numbers
Parents Without Partners International
YMCA, YWCA, or a local church or synagogue
Chemical abuse treatment centers
Chemical abuse prevention programs
Community civic centers
Women's or men's support groups
Battered women's and children's shelters
Alcoholics Anonymous, Parents Anonymous,
    and Alateen
Sexual assault centers
Local hospitals

Schools

Community education (local school district)
Colleges or universities
Community colleges
Vocational and technical schools

Government

Community mental health center or clinic
Public health nurse or department
Child protection services
Family service agencies
County social service agencies

Private Services

Psychologists, social workers, psychiatrists, therapists, family counselors

Interview the persons who will help you to see if they know about the area in which you need help. If you don't get the help you need, go somewhere else until you do.

—The Editors

How to Lead a Suggestion Circle

The Suggestion Circle is an efficient tool for collecting a variety of ideas for solving problems. It is the opposite of brainstorming.

When you are the Suggestion Circle leader, do the following:

1. Ask people to sit in a circle.
2. Tell the person who has the problem to be the "listener," to state the problem clearly and concisely. The group may ask clarifying questions.
3. Ask the person to listen to each suggestion with no comment other than a "thank-you" response.
4. Ask a group member to make a written list of the suggestions. This will allow the person to give full attention to listening to the suggestions.
5. Ask the group members to think of their best solution to the problem. Ask them to state their suggestions in one or two sentences. They are not to comment on or evaluate each other's suggestions. Go around the Circle.
6. When everyone has had a chance to give a suggestion, hand the written list of suggestions to the person with the problem to use as a resource in deciding what to do.

A Suggestion Circle of twelve people takes five minutes to complete. It is fast, caring, and efficient, and it honors everyone in the group.

A Suggestion Circle can also be done by telephone.

1. When you have a problem that you need help with, phone six friends.
2. Clearly and quickly explain the problem to each friend, and ask for his or her best suggestion. Writing the problem out before you call may help you ask more clearly.
3. Listen to the suggestion and write it down.
4. Do not comment on the suggestion, other than saying "thank you."
5. After you have phoned each friend, look over your list of suggestions and decide which to use.

—Sandra Sittko

Resources

Adams, Caren, and Fay, Jennifer. *No More Secrets*. San Luis Obispo, Calif.: Impact Publishers, 1981.

Ames, Louise B., et al. *He Hit Me First: When Brothers and Sisters Fight*. New York: Dembner Books, 1982.

Banks, Ann, and Evans, Nancy. *Goodbye, House: A Kid's Guide to Moving*. New York: Harmony Books, 1980.

Barman, Alicerose. *Helping Children Face Crises* (Public Affairs Pamphlet No. 541). Rockville, Md.: U.S. Department of Health, Education, and Welfare, 1977.

Bozarth-Campbell, Alla. *Life Is Goodbye Life Is Hello: Grieving Through All Kinds of Loss*. Minneapolis: CompCare, 1982.

Brown, Margaret. *The Dead Bird*. Reading, Mass.: Addison-Wesley Publishing Co., 1958.

Calladine, Andrew and Carole. *Raising Brothers and Sisters Without Raising the Roof*. Minneapolis: Winston Press, 1979.

Clarke, Jean Illsley. *Self-Esteem: A Family Affair*. Minneapolis: Winston Press, 1978.

_____. *Ouch. That Hurts! A Handbook for People Who Hate Criticism*. Plymouth, Minn.: Daisy Press, 1983.

_____. *The Terrific Twos* and *The Wonderful Busy Ones* (audiotapes). Minneapolis: Daisy Tapes, 16535 Ninth Avenue North, 55447, 1983.

Crary, Elizabeth. *Without Spanking or Spoiling*. Seattle: Parenting Press, 1979.

_____. *Kids Can Cooperate*. Seattle: Parenting Press, 1984.

Dads Only (monthly magazine). Julian, Calif.: Paul Lewis.

Davis, Diane. *Something Is Wrong at My House*. Seattle: Parenting Press, 1984.

Dreikurs, Rudolf. *Children: The Challenge*. New York: Hawthorn Books, 1964.

Dreikurs, Rudolf, Gould, Shirley, and Corsini, Raymond J. *Family Council: The Dreikurs Technique for Putting an End to War Between Parents and Children (and Between Children and Children)*. Chicago: Henry Regnery Company, 1974.

Elkind, David. *The Hurried Child: Growing Up Too Fast Too Soon*. Washington, D.C.: Addison-Wesley Publishing Co., 1981.

Eyre, Linda and Richard. *Teaching Children Responsibility*. Salt Lake City: Shadow Mountain, 1984.

Fassler, Joan. *My Grandpa Died Today*. New York: Human Sciences Press, 1971.

Fluegelman, Andrew. *New Games Book*. San Francisco: The Headlands Press, 1976.

Gordon, Thomas. *Parent Effectiveness Training*. New York: Peter H. Wyden, Inc., 1974.

Hendricks, Gay, and Wills, Russel. *The Centering Book*. Englewood Cliffs, N.J.: Prentice-Hall, Inc., 1975.

Hoyle, Edmund. *Hoyle's Card Games*. Boston: Routledge & Kegan Paul, 1979.

Kaufman, Gershen. *Shame: The Power of Caring*. Cambridge, Mass.: Shenkman Publishing Co., 1980.

Levin, Pamela. *Becoming the Way We Are*. Wenatchee, Wash.: Directed Media, Inc., 1974.

Maidment, Robert. *Straight Talk: A Guide to Saying More with Less*. Gretna, La.: Pelican Publishing Co., 1983.

Mayle, Peter. *What's Happening to Me?* Secaucus, N.J.: Lyle Stuart, 1975.

Newman, Susan. *Never Say Yes to a Stranger*. New York: Perigee Books, 1985.

Parents, Peers, and Pot or *Peer Pressure: It's OK to Say No*. Kensington, MD.: The National Clearinghouse for Drug Abuse Information. P.O. Box 416, 20795 (one copy free).

Piaget, Jean. *The Child and Reality*. New York: Grossman Publishers, 1973.

Rofes, Eric. *The Kids' Book of Divorce by, for and about Kids*. New York: Random House, 1982.

Snyder, Chris. *Teaching Your Child About Money*. Reading, Mass.: Addison-Wesley, 1984.

Steiner, Claude. *Warm Fuzzy Tale*. Rolling Hills Estate, Calif.: Jalmar Press, 1977.

Wachter, Oralee. *No More Secrets for Me*. Boston: Little, Brown and Co., 1983.

Zakich, Rhea. *The Ungame* (a game board with cards and playing pieces). Anaheim, Calif.: The Ungame Co., 1975.

About the Editors

Jean Illsley Clarke is the author of the book *Self-Esteem: A Family Affair* and of the parenting program of the same name. The Suggestion Circle technique comes from that program. Jean is a Transactional Analyst, a parent educator, and a mother of three. She has a Master of Arts in Human Development and an honorary Doctorate of Human Services. She likes kids this age and enjoys hassling with them.

Deane Gradous, M.B.A., is mother to a son and a daughter, both engineers. She loves and appreciates Fred, her husband of twenty-six years, also an engineer. Deane recently earned an M.B.A. and a certificate in Training and Development. She strongly advocates providing firm rules and a family structure that protects but does not bind.

Sandra Sittko, M.S.W., holds a Master of Social Work degree from the George Warren Brown School of Social Work, Washington University, St. Louis, Missouri. She leads the "Self-Esteem: A Family Affair" parenting class and uses the skills with her clients, her family, and her friends. Sandra collects rocks smoothed by the water and sand of Lake Superior and paints Affirmations on them.

As a pediatrician, **Christine Ternand**, M.D., sees twenty to thirty families daily and learns with them about human growth and development, and about parenting. She specializes in pediatric endocrinology. She uses parenting education in her practice at Group Health to help create a preventive rather than just problem-solving practice. She and her husband Doug expand their parenting skills with their two wonderful sons— Alex and Eric.

Index

132

133

Other Learning Materials Available

Developmental Tapes, by Jean Illsley Clarke. These audio cassette tapes present important information about children and the nurturing they need. Told in entertaining and easy-to-understand language from the perspective of children of different ages, the tapes describe child care by parents and by day-care providers. The stories allow adults to set aside fear or guilt and have the distance they may need to hear the information presented. The tapes, told in both male and female voices, are also useful tools for helping older children understand their little brother's and sister's needs and behavior. Each story is twelve-to-eighteen minutes long; at least eight spaced listenings are recommended.

Ups and Downs with Feelings, by Carole Gesme. This collection of games features a game board with a wide variety of "feeling faces" to help children and adults identify feelings and learn ways to be responsible for them. Included are directions for seven separate games, one of which uses the affirmations printed in this book.

Affirmation Cards. Tiny colored cards, with a separate affirmation printed on each, that can be read, carried, or given as gifts.

For more information, including prices, write to

Daisy Press
16535 Ninth Avenue North
Plymouth, MN 55447